Returning to teach in primary schools

Peter Eagling, Sylvia Turner, Charly Ryan and Doug Tanner

First published in 2002 by Learning Matters Ltd.

British Library Cataloguing in Publication Data
A CIP record for this book is available from the British Library.

ISBN 1 903300 68 1

Cover design by Topics – The Creative Partnership
Project management by Deer Park Productions
Typeset by Pantek Arts Ltd., Maidstone, Kent
Printed and bound in Great Britain by Bell & Bain Ltd, Glasgow

Learning Matters Ltd
58 Wonford Road
Exeter EX2 4LQ
Tel: 01392 215560
Email: info@learningmatters.co.uk
www.learningmatters.co.uk

CONTENTS

ACKNOWLEDGEMENTS

The authors would like to thank the following people for their advice and guidance:

Catherine Christensen (Course Administrator for Returner Teachers course, King Alfred's College Winchester), Lesley Hutchings (head teacher, Swanmore Primary School, Swanmore), Paul Key (art co-ordinator, King Alfred's College Winchester), Alison Langrish (deputy head teacher, St Monica's Junior School, Southampton), Judith McCullouch (mathematics tutor, King Alfred's College Winchester), Marilyn Manchester (deputy head, Stanmore Primary School, Winchester), David Retter (Head of Services for Pupils, Hampshire County Council), Peter Roberts (acting deputy head teacher, Oliver's Battery Primary School, Winchester), Jonathan Rooke (English tutor, King Alfred's College Winchester), Janet Sparkes (School Partnership Manager, King Alfred's College Winchester) and Mick Yates (mathematics tutor, King Alfred's College Winchester).

The authors would also like to thank Millgate House Publishers for permission to reproduce the concept cartoon in Chapter 4 from *Thinking About Science* (Keogh and Naylor, 1997) and Sophie Tierney for permission to reproduce Figure 4.2 in Chapter 4.

INTRODUCTION

This book is written for returner teachers who hope to resume work in primary schools after some years of absence from teaching. Some of you will have been trained to teach infants and juniors. Others may have trained to teach at secondary level but have decided to move to teach in the primary phase. Many returning teachers have had recent experience in primary schools through helping in their children's classes or through work as teaching assistants. In many cases, returners have left teaching in order to bring up their families or because of a career change, and now wish to return to the profession.

As tutors on the returners' course at King Alfred's College, Winchester, we have noticed a lack of books written specifically to meet your needs as returners. There are many texts giving an overview of professional matters aimed at undergraduate and PGCE students and there are a few books designed to help the newly qualified teacher. What is missing is an overview of recent developments which will help you to understand what you may experience in school today and will enable you to restart your teaching career with confidence. In this book, we explain the thinking behind recent changes so that you will feel as informed and up to date with recent educational initiatives as your colleagues, as well as offer practical classroom advice.

This book will also be useful to teaching assistants who are thinking about a career in teaching, and may be useful to postgraduates and newly qualified teachers looking for a succinct introduction to teaching today.

As a teacher, you will be expected to provide suitable learning challenges for all children, by planning effectively to overcome potential barriers to learning and by responding to diverse learning needs. Detailed guidance on inclusion and special educational needs lies beyond the scope of this text but issues to do with inclusion are touched on in each of the chapters.

Chapter 1 is a general update on primary education and gives advice about your school placement. Chapters 2 and 3 deal with English and mathematics respectively, concentrating on the recent national initiatives which have so changed the general style and approach of primary teaching. Chapter 4 deals with science and Chapter 5 covers the rest of the curriculum. The final chapters consider assessment and behaviour management. Each chapter follows a common structure: aims, suggested reading, background, current practice, preparing to teach and useful resources.

This chapter will:

- → introduce key preliminary reading;
- → familiarise you with TTA (Teacher Training Agency) requirements for school experience;
- → review a number of key issues currently facing primary teachers;
- → discuss the observation of teaching and classroom organisation;
- → consider how to work from the school's planning;
- → introduce the TTA Career Re-entry Profile.

Background reading

Before your first visit or within the first few weeks, you should obtain and selectively read from the following: *The National Curriculum: Handbook for Primary Teachers in England* (DfEE, 1999b) or *Curriculum Guidance for the Foundation Stage* (DfEE/QCA, 2000), *Special Educational Needs Code of Practice* (DfEE, 2001b), *Handbook for Inspecting Primary and Nursery Schools* (DfEE, 2000c), the school prospectus, the school's last OFSTED (Office for Standards in Education) report, recent newsletters to parents and, if it exists, the file of information for new teachers.

If you have a placement in a class from Year 1 to Year 6, you should concentrate on the first handbook; the second is for teachers in Early Years settings. Both set out principles in an introduction which repays close study. You should skim the Programmes of Study and Attainment Targets, with their levels, for the various subjects from Year 1 onwards or the six Areas of Learning for the Foundation Stage. It is important that you become familiar with the terminology and the way the material is referenced since both will feature extensively in the school's planning. School prospectuses are much more informative and professionally produced than in the past and can say a lot about the ethos and aims of the school. They frequently provide invaluable information about who is who (including teachers, administrative staff, classroom and lunchtime assistants and governors), staff responsibilities, in-house rules and other practical matters that you need to be aware of. They may also contain details of recent National Tests (often referred to as SATs) results, selections of OFSTED reports, the school's action plan and a summary of the annual report from the governors to the parents. If you have the opportunity to study a number of prospectuses, you gain an impression of the great variety that exists amongst primary schools. Since there will be children with special needs in most classes you visit, you should know about the new *Code of Practice* which emphasises that these children are the responsibility of every teacher. You should concentrate on the section on Early Years or the primary phase as appropriate. Finally, you should dip into the OFSTED *Handbook* to get a sense of what an inspection is like.

Requirements for the placement

In their specification to providers, the TTA (2002) requires that returners must spend at least a third of their course on regular school visits and states that the following should normally be planned.

- Observations of a number of lessons from the child's point of view.

- Developing planning, target setting and assessment skills.

- Observations of the range of the pupils' ability and their progression throughout the school.

- The development of behaviour management strategies.

- Observations of lessons and the day-to-day life of the school.

And, 'when participants are ready':

- team teaching with a group of pupils;

- full class teaching in one or two lessons.

Returners courses vary as to how the placement is arranged. In some cases, school(s) and mentor(s) are chosen for you, in which case you can skip the next two paragraphs! Other courses ask students to make their own arrangements, often providing an introductory letter to the head teacher, an outline of the course and a summary of TTA expectations.

Some returners find it beneficial to work in two schools – for example, an infant and a junior school or in two classes of one school. If at all possible, it helps to be able to observe in both morning and afternoon sessions since maths and English generally predominate before noon and it is also useful to make visits on different days of the week to experience different subjects. Unless there are particular reasons for it, you should avoid the school that your children attend or where you are a governor or where you are a classroom assistant since this can lead to issues of confidentiality and conflict of interest. It is, however, possible to combine supply work with further observation in the same school.

Don't be surprised if your first attempts to fix up a placement are not successful. Schools now have more visitors than ever, including work placements from secondary schools, Trident students, nursery nurse placements and many more, and it may be that an OFSTED inspection is impending. The important thing is to begin negotiations in good time and to be prepared to try a number of schools.

Before starting your visits to school you will need to undergo a police check, now known as 'enhanced disclosure', under regulations relating to the protection of children and vulnerable adults. Starting from September 2002 an application for clearance will need to be made to the Criminal Records Bureau and you need to check with your course provider whether they will organise this or whether it is your responsibility.

You should be aware that the way teaching practices are organised on under-graduate and Post-Graduate Certificate in Education (PGCE) courses has changed. In place of the flying visits of college tutors sitting at the back of the class scribbling in their notebooks, most of the supervision is done by teachers who combine sup-port and advice in their role as a 'mentor' in a partnership between schools and trainers. It is important you make clear that you will be required to take the class as a whole and that you are not a parent helper or a classroom assistant. Ask to do short whole-class activities such as taking the register, reading stories or introduc-ing a starting point for writing from an early stage of your visits. In this way, you will be seen by the class as a 'real' teacher, perhaps on a job share. Equally, when work-ing with a group, it is advisable to treat them as you would if they were part of the whole class. A 'no nonsense' approach is appropriate even in informal situations.

Background and current practice
What's in a name?

Schools for primary-aged children consist of infant schools (for children aged 4–7), junior schools (for children aged 7–11), or combined junior and infant schools, gener-ally known as primary schools, for children aged 4–11 years. An alternative system is in three tiers, with lower or first schools from 4 to 8 years or 4 to 9 years, then middle schools for 8 to 12 years or 9 to 13 years followed by upper schools.

These schools are of five main types. A majority are county schools. A number who provide facilities for the local area are designated as community schools. About a third are church schools, with the Church of England and the Roman Catholic church predominating, though recently other faith schools have been founded. Church schools are either voluntary controlled or voluntary aided, and it is in aided schools that the churches have the most influence. The fifth category is foundation schools and many of these were formerly known as grant maintained schools. You may also hear the term EAZ school, which means that it is part of an Educational Action Zone, or Beacon School, which means it is a centre of excellence.

A broad and balanced curriculum

However they are named, primary schools have changed substantially in the last 15 years. The Education Reform Act 1988 saw the introduction of the National Curriculum and the requirement for 'broad and balanced' teaching. Towards the end of the 1990s, schools were encouraged to concentrate on the core subjects and many did so at the expense of drama, music, environmental studies and other non-core activities. Other schools felt this narrowing of the curriculum was not in the children's best interests, and that a more varied and creative approach actually improved results in the core subjects. This debate is still continuing. Part of the school's responsibility is to keep parents informed about what their children are covering and how this being taught, and a range of publicity devices are used including prospectuses, termly newsletters, home pages and other means.

Local management of schools

Another change introduced by this Act was the introduction of local management of schools. The motivation for this was the then government's campaign against local authorities and its attempt to devolve power to governing boards of schools. In the primary schools of today, governors have wide-ranging powers and a prominent profile – their photographs and names are often to be found in the school entrance; they are expected to visit in school hours as well as in events after school; most governing bodies associate certain governors with specific areas of the curriculum or with particular classes; and the governors must review and approve the school's policies and action plans and a subcommittee will review the head teacher's performance. The governors will be informed of your placement in the school and may, formally, have to give their approval!

Another aspect of local management that was introduced was the relaxation of admission limits to allow open enrolment. Where parents have access to two or more primary schools for their children, this can mean declining rolls for one with a consequent loss of staff (since the number of teachers and assistants in a school is related to the total number of children on roll). Equally, when a school is oversubscribed, it can lead to appeals by disappointed parents. With this in mind, it is worth looking carefully at the admissions policy in the school prospectus.

National Tests

Commonly known as SATs, these were introduced early in the 1990s in an (initially) hostile atmosphere from teachers. They are marked externally at Key Stages 2 and 3, a considerable expense to the school, while at Key Stage 1 the internal marking is moderated outside the school. Why are the National Tests results important for a school?

First, the results at Key Stage 2 are published every year in the local and national press in the form of a league table for each local authority so parents can see the relative position of all the local schools. These results, both at Key Stages 1 and 2, are probably the most important sources of evidence that the OFSTED inspectors will review in coming to a judgement about the school. Using 'benchmarking' measures to appraise recent results (comparing the school's performance with others with a similar intake and catchment), the inspector decides whether standards are as they should be.

With so much at stake, it is not surprising that all schools ensure that pupils are familiarised with the tests and some move close to teaching to the test with the curriculum consisting of past test papers. The government would appear to sympathise with this approach with its 'booster' classes and collections of revision materials.

Inspection

All primary schools are inspected on a regular basis by OFSTED. The report of the inspection will cover:

- educational standards;

- quality of education;

- efficiency with which financial resources are managed;

- the spiritual, moral, social and cultural development of the pupils.

The report on the school will also reflect the inspection team's judgement on how well the school is led and managed by the head teacher and the governing body. Judgement is made on a seven-point scale, with 1 being 'excellent' and 7 being 'very poor'. Here is an extract from an excellent school:

> *St. Paul's Primary School is a lively and friendly community where pupils achieve very high standards in reading, writing or mathematics. The quality of teaching is excellent. The head teacher, governors, staff and parents work very hard together to achieve their simply stated aim: 'high standards for all.' The school has above average income but provides good value for money.*

> *OFSTED, 1999, p. 15.*

If, however, the judgement is that the school is not as effective as it should be, or poor or very poor, inspectors must explicitly state in their report that the school is failing to give its pupils an acceptable standard of education and thus requires special measures, or the school has serious weaknesses in one or more areas of its work or is judged to be underachieving – hence the terms 'special measures' and 'serious weaknesses'.

It is well worth skimming through the the *Handbook for Inspecting Primary and Nursery Schools* (DfEE, 2002), looking in particular at what merits praise and what leads to criticism. Consider, for example, the following:

> *Extract showing weakness in the corporate judgements in a full inspection of a junior school.*
> - *In half of 48 lessons seen, low expectations resulted in underachievement.*
> - *In all year groups English and maths work did not challenge the pupils.*
> - *In Y5 teachers praised copied work.*
> - *Parents concerned about low level of challenge for able pupils.*
> - *Little distinction in the work produced by average and high attaining pupils.*

> *OFSTED, 1999, p. 34.*

OFSTED inspectors can be breathtakingly blunt, but remember that their reports have led to improvement in the minority of failing schools and that most schools obtain satisfactory or good ratings.

Teaching assistants

In the last decade, an increasing number of paid adult helpers have worked alongside teachers in a variety of roles. Many contracts tend to be short term so there may be limited job security. There is still confusion about the titles and the acronyms that go with these – there are classroom assistants, teaching assistants, classroom learning support assistants, non-teaching assistant, special needs assistants, and supervisory assistants and old terms such as 'dinner ladies' or 'ancillary staff' persist.

From 1994 onwards, training (such as the Specialist Teacher Assistant or STA course) has been available and the 'ancillary' role has become less important than that of developing the children's learning. The assistant works with the children but the pupils are still the responsibility of the teacher.

Most teaching assistants now have job descriptions and there is a new pay structure which depends on experience, qualifications, responsibilities and hours worked. You should find out about the role of classroom assistants in your school and the ways in which teachers and assistants work together in planning and monitoring pupils' progress.

Performance management

Since 1988, the running of schools has increasingly been thought of in business terms, a process which culminated in 1999 with performance management. For teachers of a number of years of experience, there is the possibility of threshold payments which are available to those who show evidence of proficiency in stipulated aspects of teaching. The head teacher, too, is appraised by a subcommittee of governors and an external assessor for his or her success in meeting the previous targets for school improvement, his or her salary is agreed and future targets are set.

Preparing to teach
What to observe

One of the things that full-time primary teachers say is that they do not have adequate opportunities to observe and learn from other skilled practitioners. As a returning teacher you will have a unique chance to see how a number of teachers organise their day, how they get attention and maintain it, how they promote and reward acceptable behaviour, how they communicate so children listen, how they use questioning and exposition to teach and how they involve all the group or class in genuine discussion. You need to consider how you can distil what you learn from watching colleagues, what sort of records to keep and how you might use these in the future.

Again, all classes and all schools have sets of procedures, rules, routines and ways of doing things. Some of these will be explicit and may well be formalised in public notices such as 'Rules for Class 3', 'If you get stuck' or 'Nothing to do?' To show children how things are organised, the teacher will use certain semi-ritualised expressions or formulas often accompanied by set body language and a distinctive tone of voice. These will indicate the start of a session, a move from one activity to another, that the session will end shortly, the need to remember how to behave, a reminder to pay attention, a direction to think, permission to do individual work and so on. Each teacher has her or his own repertoire of set phrases, routines of behaviour and lines of thinking and these give structure to the way that children experience the school day and week. In one school, teachers tend to have a 'house style' of phrases and routines though there will be considerable variation. As a returner teacher, your task is to familiarise yourself with the contemporary language and routines of primary schools, and then to pick and mix what you have learned for your own purposes.

As a visitor, you have a privileged opportunity to observe the children's learning and the way they interact in groups and in the class. In guided writing sessions, for example, you will be able to attend closely to the responses of six children without the need to worry about the rest of the class. You should also seek opportunities to work with children on an individual basis, 'hearing' reading, giving reading or writing interviews, or talking about their understanding of an aspect of mathematics.

If you want further guidance on what to observe there are many well written guides for PGCE students, of which Hughes (2000) and Cockburn (2001) are recent examples. In Chapter 3 of the first book, Pat Hughes reviews observation of the physical environment (including risk management and safety), school groupings, class groupings, strategies for successful classroom management (including pupil involvement), minimising disruption, types of behavioural problems and strategic locations and, finally, learning areas. In Chapter 3 of the latter book, Gillian Preece covers the following topics: physical resources, rules, routines and procedures, fixed points, classroom management, teaching, movement around the classroom and asking questions and giving answers. These headings give a general indication of the kind of things to observe during your school experience.

If you come from a secondary background, you should also pay attention to child-care/pastoral matters that arise from working with younger children. What are the arrangements about the children taking medicine or using inhalers? What do you do if a child has an accident? What happens if PE kit is forgotten? What about giving the children permission to go to the toilet in lesson time? How is dinner money collected and what about lunch boxes?

If you come from a primary background, you will notice that infant and junior teachers use approaches formerly associated with secondary schools. There is far more class teaching, children are expected to sit and listen for longer periods and are expected to be able to work as independent groups while the teacher is teaching another group. This gives you a different agenda for observation.

How to observe and be observed

In order to function satisfactorily as a teacher in a school, you need to have certain key information – timetable details, names and times of classroom assistants and regular visitors, names, dates of birth and groupings of children in the class, textbooks, exercise books, how to mark, use of the photocopier and school telephone, use of the library and so on. Some of this will be in the school prospectus, some will be in the packs for new teachers or students, and some will be in the school policies which will probably be kept in the staffroom and your first task is to search this information out.

You need to agree with your class teacher/mentor the basis of your experience in the class. She or he may expect you always to help with groups but you must explain that TTA requirements of observing lessons from the child's point of view or observing the range of the pupils' ability and their progression throughout the school mean that you cannot always be interacting with children. Ask if the teacher has any objections to your making notes during her or his sessions. These are best kept to a minimum during lessons – you should use break times and after school to write them in more detail. Would she or he like to see them and discuss their contents? Whatever the response, it is advisable to write your commentary assuming it will be read by the teacher. Avoid judgemental statements and be strictly objective in what you record.

Being observed can be mildly traumatic for even the boldest of teachers, and it helps if you explain why you are keeping a record of your experiences and how you expect to use this record. Your course will give guidelines about observing behaviour management and assessment, for example. It diffuses tension if you share these with your mentor and discuss how you might write these up.

Before you teach a lesson to the class as a whole, you should watch your mentor and possibly other teachers teaching a similar lesson. There are many schedules for this, including the following suggested by Holmes (1999, p. 175):

- *How did the teacher gain the attention of the pupils?*
- *How was the lesson introduced?*
- *What motivated the pupils?*
- *How were resources used?*
- *How did the teacher employ questions?*
- *How was the lesson paced?*
- *Did the teacher respond to the needs of the pupils?*
- *What links were made to previous and future lessons?*
- *What would you have done differently and why?*

During the lesson it is particularly helpful to have a copy of the short-term plan the teacher is working from and later to set the lesson in context by looking at the mid-term plan. It is also useful to find out about any published resources being used and to look at recent work in the subject of the lesson from selected pupils.

After you have taught a number of group sessions, you will feel that you have gained the confidence to work with all the class. If your mentor gives you the choice, it is best if she or he **briefly** introduces proceedings then hands over to you. If you have agreed to teach a number of whole-class sessions, it is best if your mentor delays formal observation until the third or fourth of these. In discussing how newly quali-fied teachers (NQTs) prepare for being formally observed, Elizabeth Holmes (1999, p. 279) suggests the following:

- *Talk to your observer about the lesson you plan to teach.*
- *Give your observer all necessary documents.*
- *Decide when you can meet to discuss the feedback.*
- *Listen to the feedback carefully and accept any tips that may be offered while justifying your actions when appropriate.*

Feedback from your mentor will be an invaluable form of evidence for your Career Re-entry Profile (see below).

How to record your observations

Though it is not a formal requirement from the TTA as such, most returner courses suggest that you keep a log or diary of your school experience which will contribute to the evidence needed for your Professional Profile. In this, you should keep a record of the activities negotiated between you and your school, together with any tasks set as part of your course. In your entries you should:

- describe your observations of teachers and pupils in the classroom, together with information about the school's policies and practices;

- reflect upon your experiences in school in the light of your reading and study;

- analyse your observations and experiences according to your understanding of effective teaching and learning;

- identify the significant professional issues.

It may be that your course involves a project, an investigation or a piece of action research based on your classroom experiences, in which case you should be reflecting on possible topics and approaches from an early stage.

Whatever the format of your diary of school experience, it is important that you consider issues of confidentiality. It should not be possible to identify children, teachers or other school personnel from what you write and you should check that the copies of documents you include can be made public. You probably will need permission to photocopy children's work or take photographs of the children.

Planning

One of the effects of recurring OFSTED inspections is a greater emphasis on planning. Before the inspection, the main documentation must be made available, including the school's mission statement, policy statements and medium and long-term plans. During the inspection itself, teachers are expected to show a detailed outline to the inspector and this will be important in the assessment of the lesson. Through all this planning, schools hope to demonstrate that their pupils are receiving their entitlement of a 'broad a balanced curriculum', that the teaching and assessment are effective and that the school is giving value for money.

Ask your mentor to talk through their planning with you. Try to find the answers to the following questions.

- What is the school's approach to planning?

- What types of planning are undertaken?

- How often and for how long do staff meet to plan?

- How does the planning support the teacher and enable learning to take place?

- To what extent are pupils involved in planning their own learning?

Obtain copies of some of the main planning documents. At the top of the pyramid will be the overall statement of aims, sometimes called a mission statement, which will often appear in the school's prospectus and should reflect the ethos and nature of the school. Compare, for example, the first two aims from the prospectuses of three different kinds of primary school.

- *To develop a sense of right and wrong so children can make good choices in their lives.*
- *To support them as they seek to make Jesus someone special in their lives.*
- *To set challenging but achievable and realistic targets for all children.*
- *To enable the children to develop as confident and well balanced individuals who have a strong sense of personal achievement.*
- *To increase the children's knowledge, experience and understanding of themselves.*
- *To develop positive learning attitudes, skills and behaviour and the ability to question and argue rationally.*

Find out where these aims are to be found, whom they seem to be intended for and how they are shared. Are the aims expressed so generally that it is hard to disagree with them? How might the aims be achieved and evaluated? A concern of OFSTED is that some school's aims are so vague that they are difficult to track in curriculum planning.

Moving down the pyramid, we next consider the long-term plans. These are generally produced under the leadership of the subject co-ordinator and cover the curriculum for all year groups. They may be written for each year or, in the case of smaller schools, be two or three-year rolling programmes. Sometimes they are simply content headings under the different core and foundation subjects or there may be more detail and subjects such as humanities may be linked. They will probably include the general aims in teaching the area and a statement of the school's approach.

Mid-term plans are for a half-term or a term and are much fuller. They indicate the sequence in which the curriculum will be taught and the length of time to be spent on each section. Instead of aims there will be more specific goals which will be taken from the National Curriculum Attainment Targets or the Early Learning Goals. Most schools now use the National Literacy and Numeracy Strategies' *Frameworks* as the starting point for planning in maths and English, while many base their planning for foundation subjects on the Qualifications and Curriculum Authority (QCA) outlines (see later chapters).

Short-term plans are for the week or for the day. Most experienced primary teachers have a detailed week's plan with a brief daily plan, but NQTs tend to supplement these with separate lesson plans. Ask your mentor to show you her or his planning and, as you observe her or his teaching, study the links between her or his paperwork and what she or he does.

You will need to write and work from lesson plans and must be prepared to show them to your mentor or a senior member of staff before you teach the class. They will form useful evidence in your Career Re-entry Profile.

Daily plans

The daily plan may:

- list the day's activities, including lessons, breaks, etc. with time slots;
- show planning for other adults in the classroom and contingency plans in the case of their absence;
- include class management activities such as registration, collecting money, changing for PE;
- note external events such as visitors, health checks, extra or cancelled assemblies;
- indicate the student teacher's non-teaching activities;
- include notes for activities not indicated by lesson plans – e.g. 'settling' activities, stories shared, etc.

Example of daily plan

> 9.00 Register. **Collect money for trip.**
>
> 9.10 Assembly – long assembly – Vicar.
>
> 9.45 Numeracy.
>
> 10.45 Break.
>
> 10.50 Literacy hour – me to lead. **No Mrs Blunt today, so change blue group's task.**
>
> 12.10 ...

Lesson plans

The lesson plan shows the detail of what and how something will be taught. It may be for a whole-class activity or for groups, when it may be used on more than one occasion. Your lesson plan may look something like Figure 1.1. Further guidance on how to plan and evaluate is given in Holmes (1999), Hughes (2000) and Hayes (2001).

Date	Time

Duration (National Curriculum, National Literary Strategy or National Numeracy Strategy, as appropriate.)

Title

Learning objectives *or* **intended learning outcomes**
(These should relate directly to medium-term plans and should indicate what, as a result of the activity, the pupils should know, understand and do. You should have no more than four learning objectives.)

Resources needed
(Including advanced preparation required and health and safety considerations.)

Differentiation
(How the task will be modified to meet children's individual needs; supporting children with Individual Educational Plans (IEPs) and extending the learning of more able children; use of other adults and helpers.)

Monitoring, assessing and recording
(Including which children will be assessed; which aspects of the work will be assessed; assessment strategies used, e.g. observation of children's behaviour, discussion with children, reviewing and/or marking outcomes; recording format.)

Organisation and management of learning
(Details should include:
- how you are going to start the session – including sharing the objective(s);
- how you will manage transition;
- how you will end the lesson;
- groupings and other adults/helpers involved;
- establishment of ground rules and expectations for behaviour and standards;
- initial stimulus and vocabulary to be used;
- how to phrase instructions, explanations and questions;
- plans for early finishers and those who have not yet finished;
- timings and routine for finishing, including plenary, reviews, clearing away.)

Lesson evaluation
(Consider the effectiveness of:
- planning;
- organisation;
- management of pupils' behaviour;
- use of teaching time, resources and other adults;
- use of assessment to inform planning.

To what extent did pupils:
- demonstrate interest and enjoyment in their learning?
- work effectively with others?
- take some responsibility for organising and developing their own learning?

What are the implications of your evaluation for future teaching?)

Figure 1.1 A sample lesson plan

Elizabeth Holmes (1999, pp. 213–14) writes for NQTs but much of her book is relevant for returners, including the following tips.

- *Talk to your mentor about your preparation and marking. Are you overdoing it? Are there shortcuts you should be taking? Do you know when to stop?*
- *Keep good records of your planning for the next time you cover the topic.*
- *If a textbook covers a topic well, use it rather than create your own worksheets.*

Career Re-entry Profile for returning teachers

This profile begins by saying:

All teachers are entitled to structured support, and especially on their return to teaching. Newly qualified teachers arrive in their first post with a Career Entry Profile and this helps them to make the transition from initial teacher training to becoming established teachers. It also helps schools to provide the support and monitoring that the newly qualified teacher needs.

The issues for those who have completed a career break are similar; they require and deserve support from colleagues.

The Profile for Career Re-entry can be helpful as a framework against which returning teachers can plan their professional development for their return and throughout their careers.

There are two principal purposes for the Career Re-entry Profile. First, you can use it to give information about your strengths and your development needs. Secondly, you can use it to prioritise your future professional development needs, targeting the areas where you will look for assistance in the early period of your return to teaching.

The Career Re-entry Profile has three sections.

1. Summary of the returning teacher's initial teacher training, teaching experience to date and returners' course, including any distinctive features of his or her training and any other relevant information.

2. Summary of the returning teacher's strengths and areas for further professional development.

3. Action plan, including objectives for the first few months of the position being taken.

You should bear in mind that recently qualified teachers have been required to take skills tests in English, maths and ICT. Returning teachers do **not** have to pass these but you will be expected to have the requisite subject knowledge and your profile should reflect this.

Alongside the profile, you should keep a file maintaining a record of your experiences and achievements during your school visits. This might contain lesson plans and evaluations, accounts of group work in core and foundation subjects (for example guided writing sessions) and reports of interactions with individual children (for example reading interviews or hearing reading). It might include photographs of displays you contributed to or of models the children made under your guidance. If you have helped with school clubs, games or activities, it is worth keeping a record of these. Your file could prove a useful resource during job interviews.

Summary

- Make sure that your class teacher is clear about your role in school and knows about the TTA requirement that, in time, you will be teaching the class as a whole.

- Obtain official and other information about the school as soon as possible and study it carefully.

- Make clear to your teacher that you need a balance of practical involvement and the opportunity to experience group and class work as a detached observer.

- Decide on the form of diary/log at an early stage, keep your teacher informed about what you are recording and treat it as a public document.

- Consider how your log can contribute to your Career Re-entry Profile.

- Make an early start on this profile.

Useful resources

Cockburn, A (2001) *Teaching Children 3 to 11*. London: Paul Chapman.

DfEE (1999) *The National Curriculum: Handbook for Primary Teachers in England*. London: HMSO.

Farrell, M (1999) *Key Issues for Primary Schools*. London: Routledge.

Hayes, L (2001) *Am I Teaching Well?* Exeter: Learning Matters.

Holmes, E (1999) *Handbook for Newly Qualified Teachers*. London: HMSO.

Hughes, P (2000) *Principles of Primary Education: Study Guide*. London: David Fulton.

Jacques, K (2000) *Professional Studies Primary Phase*. Exeter: Learning Matters.

OFSTED (1999) *Handbook for Inspecting Primary and Nursery Schools*. London: HMSO.

besd.becta.org.uk BECTA information about software.

www.dfes.gov.uk/index.htm DfES links to National Curriculum online and OFSTED.

www.qca.org.uk/index.asp QCA school curriculum and associated assessments.

www.tes.co.uk *The Times Educational Supplement*.

www.canteach.gov.uk/ (TTA) the teacher training community online.

etc.ngfl.gov.uk/index.html The Virtual Teacher's Centre.

This chapter will:

→ introduce key preliminary reading;

→ explain the thinking behind the Literacy Hour;

→ make you familiar with the parts of the hour and their different procedures;

→ give guidance on how to teach the hour, with suggestions for further study.

Background reading

You should obtain and read selectively from the following: *Curriculum 2000: Handbook for Teachers* (DfEE, 1999c), *The National Literacy Strategy: Framework for Teaching* (DfEE, 1998b), the English section of the Foundation Stage profile (formerly known as the baseline test) and the 2002 English National Test paper for Key Stages 1 and 2.

You should read the English section of *Curriculum 2000* and, in the *Framework*, you should study Sections 1 and 4 and the term's outline in Section 2 that applies to your class.

You should also study the Foundation Stage profile and a recent English National Test paper for Key Stages 1 and 2. These will give you an introduction to the levels of work that are now expected and you will begin to see what teachers are working towards in English lessons.

Background

> There has never been a major national initiative to enable all primary teachers to learn the most effective methods of teaching literacy and how to apply them . . . it will be the most ambitious attempt ever in this country to changes for the better teaching approaches across the entire education service.

> *DfEE, 1997, paras. 26 and 27.*

Your starting point is to read the English section of *Curriculum 2000: Handbook for Teachers* (DfEE, 1999c) because this is the legal basis for all the English teaching in the school and the Office for Standards in Education (OFSTED) inspector will use this section to base his or her judgement about the school's performance in English. The handbook sets out the curriculum for speaking and listening, reading and writing with the Attainment Targets for these three areas which go from Level 1 to 6 and give a useful guide to the levels you should expect in English. You will find many references to this document in the school's planning.

Next you should study the introduction to the *Framework*. This has **not** replaced the National Curriculum for English which remains an essential guide for overall aims in English and is particularly useful for those aspects of English teaching that lie outside the Literacy Hour, notably talking and listening. The *Framework* has, however, become the means by which most of the National Curriculum for English is now delivered and is more frequently referred to.

For someone returning to the primary classroom, one of the most obvious changes you will notice is the way that English is taught. Infants no longer queue to be 'heard' reading from the *Ginn 360* or *One, Two, Three and Away*, nor do they write news or dictate a sentence about their drawing to be copied later. 'Creative writing' and periods of silent reading are less frequent and many teachers find it hard to fit in the regular reading of a serialised story.

Instead we have the Literacy Hour with Big Books, the use of the overhead projectors or flipcharts so the whole class can participate in shared reading or writing. When the hour starts, it is normal for the teacher to share the outcomes for the session and, as it closes, it is customary to get the children to review their progress. For many teachers of younger children a relatively new item of classroom equipment is the pointer, often a stick or equivalent, to keep the children's place during oral reading or to point out features of the text. We now have texts for group reading in sets or six or eight and many schools use recently published textbooks, which support individual and group work.

Why was the Literacy Hour brought in? In the early 1990s, there was serious concern about standards in British schools. International surveys showed that, though our most able children could compete with the rest of the world on equal terms, the bottom third, the so-called 'long tail' of underachievement, compared very poorly (Brooks, 1998).

To raise standards, the current government introduced the National Literacy Project (NLP) in 1994, targeting selected schools in a number of local authorities where pupils were underachieving in literacy. The NLP was directed by John Stannard who produced a programme which gave teachers more specific guidance on what to teach in English and how to teach English than had been available before. The NLP set out a detailed series of age-related objectives together with specification of the kinds of texts to be studied and recommended the use of a predictable and unvaried routine for work in English with a four-part lesson structure.

Results of the NLP were so impressive that, in 1998, the incoming Labour government adopted the programme virtually unchanged and made it part of its National Literacy Strategy (NLS) in the drive to raise standards. Its scheme of work was republished as the *Framework*. On page 9 of this document is a diagram familiarly known as 'the clock' which shows the structure of the Literacy Hour with its sections of 15 minutes (whole class – text work), 15 minutes (whole class – word or sentence work), 20 minutes (group and independent work) then 10 minutes (whole class – review of teaching points) (Figure 2.1). This is the pattern all primary teachers have to follow when they teach English though some latitude is allowed since the abbreviation 'approx' comes after each of the timings. Many teachers and head teachers have been very concerned at the sedentary nature of the first 30 minutes, which is another reason why they departed from the timings.

Though the NLS does not have statutory force, the government encouraged schools to adopt it and only a few have opted out from using it. The government went on to target that, by 2002, 80 per cent of 11-year-olds would achieve a Level 4 pass. In the first three years of the strategy, dramatic improvements were recorded, particularly in reading and particularly by the girls. In 2001 the results

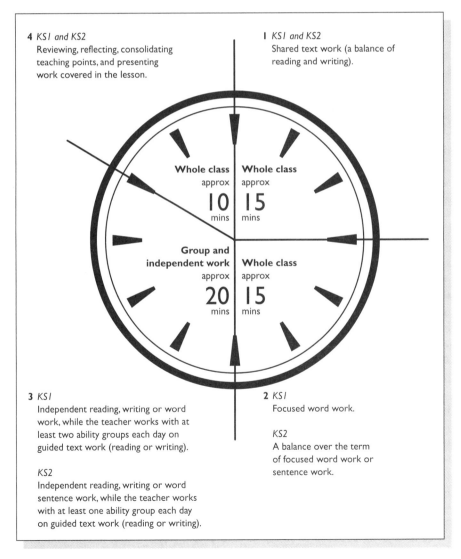

4 *KS1 and KS2*
Reviewing, reflecting, consolidating teaching points, and presenting work covered in the lesson.

1 *KS1 and KS2*
Shared text work (a balance of reading and writing).

Whole class approx **10 mins**

Whole class approx **15 mins**

Group and independent work approx **20 mins**

Whole class approx **15 mins**

3 *KS1*
Independent reading, writing or word work, while the teacher works with at least two ability groups each day on guided text work (reading or writing).

KS2
Independent reading, writing or word sentence work, while the teacher works with at least one ability group each day on guided text work (reading or writing).

2 *KS1*
Focused word work.

KS2
A balance over the term of focused word work or sentence work.

Figure 2.1 The 'clock'

flattened out with the overall results in writing and the performance by the boys being less than was hoped for. None the less, quite remarkable progress had been achieved and, in 2002, the target was been revised upwards so that, by 2004, 85 per cent should achieve a Level 4 pass and 35 per cent are to attain a Level 5.

What are the principles behind the Literacy Hour? First, from 1990 onwards there was a change in view about the merits of class teaching compared with the limitations of working with children on an individual basis or in groups and a reappraisal of the benefits of direct instruction compared to the inefficiency of discovery methods (Alexander, 1992). From its inception, the teacher was to *teach* throughout the Literacy Hour.

The aim of this teaching was to produce children who were able to read and write independently, and the structure of the hour is designed to move pupils towards independence. In the shared section, there is a lot of support and the teacher is doing most of the work; in guided sessions, the children have to do more on their own, leading to largely independent work in groups or as individuals. In a recent survey it was found that a significant number of teachers had not grasped this principle and some would not plan for pupils to work independently. Best progress was found where teachers had deliberately fostered the ability of children to work on their own (Fisher, 2002, p. 165).

It is also important to *demonstrate* the skills of reading and writing. If you hear something explained, you will probably forget it, but if you see it being done **then** have it explained, you may well remember it. How does a beginner learn a complex skill like reading or writing? The teacher has to show what is involved, if necessary, 'in slow motion', making what is unconscious in skilled performance explicit. To use a psychological term, this is teaching meta-cognition or, more simply, 'wondering aloud'. It was precisely this ability to wonder aloud (i.e. to talk about how they set about reading or writing) that picked out the most successful teachers in Fisher's survey (Fisher, 2002, p. 165).

And for meta-cognition to take place about reading and writing, it is necessary to have technical vocabulary, in other words, a meta-language. In order to think about phonics, children need to know terms like 'syllable' or 'phoneme', which are now commonplace among Year R pupils. In order that juniors can write in a more varied way, they need to know the difference between compound and complex sentences. At the end of the *Framework* you will find a glossary of technical terms that primary children (and their teachers!) are expected to be familiar with.

In devising the overall approach, Stannard introduced two key ideas. From Marilyn Jaeger Adams (1994) he derived the notion of 'level'. In the USA, Adams had reviewed the advantages and disadvantages of various methods of the teaching of reading. Was the 'top down' emphasis more effective than a 'basic skills' approach? Adams concluded that an approach that combined phonics with an emphasis on context and meaning was overwhelmingly the most effective. From this came the strategy's 'levels' of reading and writing that are integral to how the Literacy Hour is taught: work at word level concentrates on phonics and spelling; work at sentence level is about grammar and punctuation; and work at text level is about the 'bigger shapes' (e.g. genre, characterisation, story, grammar and style).

From Marie Clay (1979), he derived the notion of 'searchlights'. Clay had achieved spectacular results with her 'reading recovery' method in New Zealand. It worked because it taught children to read and write using all the strategies available to them. Stannard adopted this all-round approach, and page 4 of the *Framework* shows a diagram of the 'searchlights' of phonics, word recognition, grammatical knowledge and use of context, which are at the heart of the Literacy Hour (see Figure 2,2). Why did Stannard use the term 'searchlights'? As a child he had experienced the air raids on London and had seen how German planes could be pinpointed when they were caught in the beams of two or more searchlights. In the same way, it is argued, use of all possible strategies will lead to success in reading and writing.

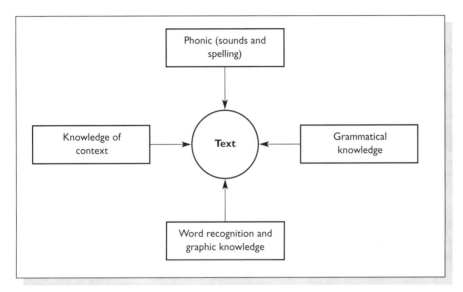

Figure 2.2 The reading searchlights

How was the NLS implemented? A distance-learning pack (popularly known as the 'lunch box') was distributed to all primary schools. It consisted of training manuals covering the main aspects of the Literacy Hour supported by audio and video tapes, and training days were allocated for schools to master this material. Though some of the teaching shown now seems somewhat joyless, the videos are still well worth watching.

Local authorities appointed teachers as literacy consultants to lead the training of head teachers and language consultants and to go round schools giving demonstration lessons and advising on organisation and resources.

The NLS has maintained a steady stream of handbooks and video training tapes to supplement the *Framework*, including an excellent publication on the teaching of phonics, *Progression in Phonics* (DfEE, 1999a), two indispensable handbooks for teaching writing, *Grammar for Writing* (DfEE, 2000b) and *Developing Early Writing* (DfEE, 2001a), a guide on the teaching of spelling and various remedial packages. Also worth consulting are the Key Stage 2 Spelling Bank and the grammar and writing fliers.

This is a good time to be learning how to teach the Literacy Hour since research suggests that it has, in general, gained acceptance from most primary teachers, though there are reservations about particular aspects (Earl, 2001). Many teachers will tell you that it has extended their understanding of how children learn to read and write and has given them a new range of strategies for teaching English. It may seem daunting at first but it is worth sticking with.

Current practice
Shared reading at text level

At Key Stage (KS) 1 the teacher will choose a short, predictable story, poem or non-fiction text, often with a refrain for joining in. On day one, the teacher shows the front cover and some of the pictures and invites predictions. He or she then reads and perhaps re-reads with a few children joining in pointing as he or she reads. On day two, the teacher recapitulates the text then re-reads, this time leading most of the class in chorus then develops the children's response to the story – how would you feel if this happened to you? What can you tell from the pictures and so on? After some writing based on the text in day three, we return to the story on day four. After further recapitulation, there will be confident chorus reading then perhaps some solo performance from volunteers, the class taking it in turn to read, following the teacher's reading without the pointer or some silent reading.

The approach is based on the 'story method' of learning to read which was popularised by Don Holdaway in the 1970s (Holdaway, 1979). The children virtually memorise a text then figure out the relationship between what they are looking at and what they are saying, using the searchlights of word recognition, phonics, grammar and context. Once they have gained confidence in the context of the story, the children can go on to work at the mechanics of reading, mainly at word level.

At KS2, it is assumed that most children can decode so the emphasis is on 'reading in the mind' – that is, reading to learn or reading reflectively. It used to be thought that, once children had finished their reading scheme, they could be let loose as 'free range' readers and no further teaching was necessary. We now know there are further skills to be developed. Consider, for example, how you would use an encyclopaedia to find out about the diet of a dinosaur or how you worked out precisely what the genre was of the first *Harry Potter* book you read (Rowling, 1997). In junior classes, the role of the teacher is to demonstrate reflective reading 'in slow motion' and to show how the text works. Just as a skilled guide can bring a work of art to life and make you see things you were unaware of, so the teacher can develop children's understanding of fiction and non-fiction and their response to text. To understand some of the advanced processes of reading it helps to give them a name, and some of the teaching will be directed towards terms such as 'flashback', 'report', 'atmosphere' or 'instructions'. The teacher will follow these up in the writing sessions that follow.

At KS2, more use is made of extracts, and Big Books may be used less than enlarged photocopies, overhead transparencies (OHTs) or multiple copies of the text. Sometimes, the teacher will read the passage aloud, with the class following; sometimes an audio tape can be used, volunteers can read parts of the text but more of the reading will be silent. Part of the craft of teaching is to break up the text into manageable chunks and to bear in mind the varying reading speeds and comprehension levels of the class. Look out for evidence of the huge range of speed and concentration in silent reading in your class and reflect on how the teacher copes with this. KS2 classes are often taught as ability sets, wherever this is possible. As one teacher comments:

> Ability setting allows children to be taught at their own level, rather than the 'Third Reich' approach of 'you are now in Y6 and we will teach you subordinate verbs even though you can't spell your name!'

Consider, too, that the collective concentration of a whole-class reading is a fragile matter, easily punctured.

Shared reading at word and sentence level

In the next section of the hour the teacher will work with the class at reading skills that can generally be practised in the text that has been shared. These will come from the term's outline in the *Framework* and the texts studied will be probably have been selected with these objectives in mind. For instance, *The Cat in the Hat* (Seuss, 1958) would be a natural choice for developing awareness of rhyme and analogy, whereas the opening of *Charlotte's Web* (White, 1952) would be a good place to find sentence-level work on punctuating dialogue.

Teachers have begun to experiment with the order of this part of the hour and it is quite acceptable, on occasions, to start the hour with this section or to inter-weave your word and sentence work with the work at text level in a half-hour block. It is sometimes difficult to find a connection between the objectives to be covered and the texts you have to use, in which case, do not attempt it but teach the skills section separately.

A criticism sometimes made of the shared section is that there is too much teacher talk and not enough interaction. In fact, the NLS advice is to get the children talking in pairs or small groups, to involve them in activities such as hot-seating, role play and human sentences and to have interactive materials such as show me cards, letter or other fans, washing lines and whiteboards. Flier I (DfEE, 1999d) gives the following advice:

- *Ask authentic questions.*
- *Stay open to unexpected ideas.*
- *Show interest in what the children* think *not just in what they know.*
- *Let what the children say affect the course of discussion.*

One important thing to be aware of is that greater demands are now made on teachers' knowledge than in the past, and you will need to familiarise yourself with the linguistic terms you will be teaching. A useful starting point is the revised glossary for the NLS which can be downloaded from the NLS website. If you lack confidence on grammar, *Collins Grammar Rules* (Rose, 1997) is an unthreatening introduction, though you should buy a more substantial text such as Crystal (1996) or Medwell (2002) at a later stage. In recent years there have been significant developments in research into phonics (e.g. onset and rime) and grammar (e.g. cohesion). The NLS is based on a considerable body of research (Beard, 1999). To teach it effectively you should understand its main thrust.

The *Framework* covers a wonderful range of fiction, non-fiction and poetry with which it should be hard to fail to engage your class. You will need to broaden your knowledge of these and gain an understanding of the theories about genre that underpin the strategy. The NLS have produced a first-rate series of fliers giving pithy summaries of some of the main types of fiction and non-fiction with practical advice on how to approach them (DfEE, 2000b). But listen to Gervase Phinn's (2000) advice on this point:

> *The Literacy Hour is not about going through a minimum number of texts in maximum, pleasure destroying detail, interrogating the writing in such a way that children are turned off books and reading.*

Phinn, 2000, p. 14.

Incidentally, one of the best guides about choosing good texts for the Literacy Hour is by this author.

Guided reading

Guided reading has replaced hearing children read on an individual basis in many schools. Children are grouped on the basis of their reading ability, normally in a group of six. Each child has a copy of the text, which is chosen to be at instructional level (about 90 per cent accuracy). Before the session, the teacher will have chosen particular reading strategies to work on based on the group's previous performance. The teacher leads the session, preparing the children for reading, reinforcing reading strategies and giving attention to individuals as they read the text on their own. The aim of every guided reading session is to extend independent reading.

There are a number of different ways in which the reading can take place. The children may read around the group though this should not be the norm − some children find it embarrassing or boring and it leads to the practice of guessing when it is going to be your turn. The children may read in chorus with the teacher, they may read aloud 'in broken pace', they may subvocalise but the aim is that they should read silently as soon as they can and for as long as they can. One useful practice is to have the children read silently but, when the teacher kneels down by a child, they start to read aloud.

Fisher's research (2002) shows that teachers find guided reading the most difficult part of the hour to operate and a number abstain from doing it. Others use English time outside the hour to work with children in this way. Some schools feel that the regular, one-to-one contact with an adult is essential, particularly with younger readers, and a rota is made of parents, volunteers and teaching assistants to provide individual practice. Fountas (1997) gives comprehensive advice on the theory and practice and the NLS has some useful video programmes with demonstration lessons.

Independent work in reading

This is perhaps the most difficult part of the hour to organise well and there is relatively little advice in the NLS publications though they have provided many good materials for pupils. Two points need to be made. First, the success of these sessions will depend on the training the children have received in working independently: pupils need to have had a clear explanation of what is to be done, perhaps with an aide-memoire in the form of a group card or a wall poster. They also need to feel that the work will be followed up.

Secondly, many teachers now have all independent groups working on a common task differentiated according to the ability of the children. To manage a carousel of different activities while trying to concentrate on guided reading is too frazzling and, on the principle of economy of effort, it is best to adopt the more straightforward mode of organisation.

A criticism often made of this part of the hour is that it does not provide adequate practice time and leads to a lot of unfinished work. This is to misunderstand how the Literacy Hour works as a whole. Before the strategy was introduced, in an hour's lesson, teachers would introduce a reading or writing task in 15 or so minutes then go round the class, interacting briefly and generally at a low level; such teaching as there was generally was 'after the event' – i.e. too little and too late. With the hour, children should not flounder in independent work since the ground should have been prepared in the shared part. Further, there is no reason why children should not return to the same task in a series of group-work sessions during the week.

Shared writing at word, sentence and text level

Shared writing follows naturally on from shared reading and draws on what has been done. It was first used in the 1980s with groups of less able children where the teacher would scribe their suggestions to build up their confidence and sense of story while the rest of the class were working independently. It was then introduced into infant classes as one of the ways of teaching writing. The NLS have published two handbooks to help teachers in this aspect of the Literacy Hour and you should familiarise yourself with the introductions and some of the teaching suggestions from either *Developing Early Writing* (DfEE, 2001a) or *Grammar for Writing* (DfEE, 2000b).

The main advice from these handbooks is as follows.

- Work with the whole class, to model, explore and discuss the choices writers make at the point of writing rather than by correction.

- Make the links between reading and writing explicit.

- Scaffold some aspects of writing so children can concentrate on how to compose.

- Introduce appropriate technical language as a means of discussing what writers do.

The NLS approach to writing has much in common with the 'process' approach of Donald Graves (1983); writing is seen not as a once-and-for-all matter but involves planning, drafting, editing and perhaps publishing. It also involves thinking about the purpose of the writing, the likely audience and the layout and format – in short, about the genre that is used. A shared writing session is an ideal opportunity for the teacher to show these processes at work. First, she or he will model the kind of writing to be attempted and will pretend to compose in an impromptu way, with crossings out, additions, changes of order and so on. She or he gives a running commentary as she or he writes and invites comment and opinion.

The next phase is to ask the class to continue, at first orally, when the teacher may scribe some of the suggestions. The class may then work in pairs on a whiteboard, perhaps composing a short piece such as part of a dialogue or the start of an advertisement. This is the springboard for the independent or guided writing part of the hour and enables the teacher to teach writing before the event rather than, as used to happen, leaving the improvement until it was too late, (i.e. after the writing had been completed).

One of the reported difficulties about writing in the Literacy Hour is that children do not have sufficient practice time and rarely finish a piece satisfactorily. Does your school allow opportunities for extended writing – perhaps an entire session per week or fortnight? Can the children work on their writing in the group work over a number of days, continuing and improving one piece? Are there opportunities for book-making, fiction and non-fiction? Are special audiences devised (for instance, pen pals from another school, parents, children's writers, local councillors and so on)?

Fisher (2002) found that one of the factors that picked out the better teachers of writing in her survey was their ability to demonstrate how they would write and talk to their classes about this writing. She also found that the more successful teachers had a good sense of what their pupils could achieve in writing and how to bring them on. Incidentally, the NLS has developed a valuable repertoire of tactics for improving writing, ranging from 'powerful verbs', 'showing not telling', the use of cliff-hangers and other narrative devices to using dialogue to drive a story forward. You should familiarise yourself with these.

Guided writing

The principles of guided writing are similar to those of guided reading. This is the time for work on the processes of writing – the planning or revising stages, for example. Teachers need to build up a sense of the repertoire of skills that a good writer possesses in the same way that Southgate (1981) suggested they should for reading. While talking to and observing the guided group, the teacher can develop the use of some of the repertoire, for example with narratives.

- To identify and use simple plot structures.

- To recognise and imitate different narrative openings (e.g. events, dilemmas and cliff-hangers).

- To drop in clues to suggest the ending.

A number of recent publications provide stimulating extracts to work from and give good suggestions for work in guided sessions. Examples include *The Oxford Literacy Web* (Medwell, 2000) and *Focus English* (Bennett, 2000).

Independent work in writing

OFSTED (1999, paras. 82 and 83) were unimpressed by much of the work that children produced when working on their own:

> Too much of this writing (from group and independent work) was low level at best and consisted of ... an undemanding task involving little more than copying from a simple text or filling in gaps in a worksheet.

The Strategy's advice for independent work in writing is similar to that for reading. Its success depends on preliminary teaching where the shared work acts as a scaffold for what is to follow.

Examples of such scaffoldings include:

- a variation of a well-known story;
- a partially written text to be 'infilled';
- a diagram for which instructions can be added.

Using this general pattern of support, teachers can move children to increasing independence, gradually removing the supports. It must be remembered that there is no previous shared writing support for the KS2 writing tests where pupils have to write for 45 minutes on a choice of four subjects after 15 minutes to choose and plan. With this in mind, many schools use similar lengths of time either from a Literacy Hour or out of the remaining English time.

The plenary session

During this part of the hour, the teacher checks whether the children have met the objectives set out at the beginning and invites them to reflect on what has been learned. Emphatically, it is not a 'show and tell' time and many teachers find that the most effective way to use the plenary is to timetable groups in turn so that over the week everyone gets a turn. The plenary can become very formulaic so look for ways of ringing the changes in the way it is delivered. A very effective plenary is to utilise some of the searching questions on NLS flier 1, as they prompt the children to reflect; the Hampshire County Council *Able Children* handbook (HIAS, 2000) also has very useful questions for use at different stages of lessons which can boost meta-cognitive processes.

English outside the Literacy Hour

It is of no use to teach children skills of reading and writing if they do not choose, in Frank Smith's words, to join the 'Literacy Club' (Smith, 1978). Before the NLS, primary schools worked hard to motivate children with school bookshops, author visits, frequent silent reading sessions, poetry weeks, book-making, letter exchanges and so on.

Is there time for these sorts of activities in today's pressurised atmosphere? The answer is that time must be made. In the words of *English in the National Curriculum* (DES, 1989a, p. 29):

> Children should encounter an environment in which they are surrounded by books, presented in an attractive and inviting way.

> Teaching . . . should ensure that pupils regularly hear stories told or read aloud, and hear and share poetry read by the teacher and each other.

In schools where the subject is well taught, teachers will strive to preserve the motivational aspects of past practice alongside the strengths of the strategy and will link English work in English outside the hour (including in the foundation subjects) with work in the hour. At the time of writing, there is a big drive to link foundation subjects and core English together more effectively, trying to ensure that teachers and pupils do not see them in separate compartments. Many of the non-fiction skills can effectively be practised in, for example, history or geography: learning these subjects is, partly, learning to read and write about these subjects.

Preparing to teach
How do I prepare myself to teach the Literacy Hour?

As a returning teacher, you will be expected to teach or help with part or all of the Literacy Hour, initially following the planning of your class teacher but later doing some of the planning for yourself. How should you prepare yourself for this?

The first thing to do is to watch a number of Literacy Hours, observing the class as a whole, then different groups and individuals, noting how the teacher uses other adults, particularly the teaching assistant or SNA. If possible, observe on different days and find out how the teaching is structured over the week. At an early stage it is likely that you will be asked to work with a group, but make sure you have an opportunity to observe the teacher taking guided reading or writing.

The next task is to find out about the resources for literacy teaching in the school. Look for the section of the staff library that has government and other publications that give guidance about teaching literacy. Much can be learned from the handbooks to schemes such as the *Handbook to the Oxford Literacy Web* (Gaines, 2000) or from guides such as *Choosing Texts for the National Literacy Strategy* (Lazim, 2000) and *Guiding Reading* (Hobsbaum, 2002).

Where and how are the Big Books kept and how are they catalogued and accessed? In a large school, how do teachers timetable the use of these and other new resources so they are not all needed at once? Does the school use other means of enlarging text such as overhead projectors or data projectors? Find where the sets of guided and group reading books and the English textbooks for group and individual work are kept and how they are used. Does the school use other sources of text for its individual and group work?

Other relevant resources include phonic and word recognition games, computer programs for reading, writing and spelling, CD-ROMs, information books of all kinds, audio tapes, tape recorders and video tapes (e.g. serialisations of children's stories or documentaries about well-known children's writers or poets).

How do I plan and keep records for the Literacy Hour?

The point of departure will be the relevant page from the *Framework*. Then you should ask to see the medium-term plan which will be the school's reworking of the *Framework*'s outline. Your teacher or the teachers of the year group will have a week or fortnightly plan; in some cases this is a very full document and only brief notes are needed for the daily lesson plan; in other cases, teachers have to write a daily lesson plan setting out objectives for each part of the Literacy Hour. You should ask to see these documents and other relevant information (e.g. the school's teaching guidelines for English), which may record staff discussion on aspects of the Literacy Hour. When it was introduced, some teachers found that the *Framework* led to fragmented and whistle-stop teaching with too many bits and pieces and lots of unfinished work. How coherent is the planning you are scrutinising? The current NLS advice is to block units of work together, to link current teaching objectives with ones previously taught and not to spend equal time on all objectives, moving more swiftly over those that have covered in previous terms.

When you feel ready to teach a Literacy Hour, you can find advice about content and format from some of the Post-Graduate Certificate in Education (PGCE) handbooks listed at the end of the chapter, and a number of websites publish lesson plans and activities for literacy (see below).

In most schools, there will be agreed organisational procedures for the Literacy Hour which may well have been discussed at staff meetings or on in-service days and these may be written up in the curriculum guidelines for English. Is there a school agreement about routines and behaviour during the hour? Does each class have a literacy noticeboard displaying information in a given way? Notice also how the teacher has to prepare for the lesson and consider the training that is necessary for it to run smoothly.

The NLS has been criticised for its 'bitty' approach to English. In your class, is there adequate time for children to write at length or to read for pleasure? Does the planning in your school allow these things to happen?

The next consideration is record-keeping. How does your class teacher keep a note of what he or she has taught, how the different parts of the sessions went, what was covered and, most importantly, what progress the children made? It is particularly in the guided parts of the hour that this record-keeping should go on. How detailed is it and does it feed in to future teaching?

What about children with special needs?

You need to observe carefully how your class teacher uses the Special Needs Assistant to help with children who have special needs in both the shared and guided parts of the hour. Is there an introductory session for the special needs group before the material is introduced to the whole class? Is there a 'catch up' session after? Do the children with special needs always stay with the rest of the class? In shared work, how does the teacher include all children – with differentiated questions, materials and activities, for example? What routines and reward systems are in place to help with sustained concentration and acceptable behaviour? The NLS has produced a useful handbook on this topic (DfEE, 2000a) and the three books by Sylvia Edwards (1999a, 1999b, 1999c) contain much useful advice.

How can I use ICT in the Literacy Hour?

For schools fortunate enough to possess them, data projectors are invaluable as 'electronic whiteboards' for shared reading and writing. Children will mainly be using ICT in the 20 minutes of guided and independent time. Look out for computer activities that contribute to word-level work (for example, handwriting software, spell checkers, visual discrimination games, observation and memory games and so on). At sentence level, look out for word banks or concept keyboards. At text level, there are the very popular talking books, text disclosure and cloze programs, a class database, web pages and many others. Phil Poole (2001) is a recommended source of information.

Other questions to think about

- How do you establish a sense of ownership over the NLS?
- Does it matter if you go over time?
- Doesn't the Literacy Hour stifle creativity?
- How do you avoid unfinished work?
- Why are there so many technical terms?

Hopefully, you will have found the seeds of the answers to these questions in this chapter!

Summary

- The National Literacy Strategy is a means of delivering the National Curriculum for English; it does not replace the National Curriculum.
- Some aspects of English will be taught outside the Literacy Hour.
- The *Framework* of the NLS does not address speaking and listening.
- The NLS is not part of a 'back to basics' movement but draws on a broad survey of recent research into literacy and learning.
- It emphasises context and meaning together with phonics and word recognition.

- It has introduced new vocabulary and teaching procedures into the teaching of English.

- Teachers and children work in different ways in different parts of the hour.

- The timings of the parts of the hour are approximate.

- Teachers who use the NLS are most successful if they internalise the objectives of the *Framework* and have their own style of delivering these.

Useful resources

Bentley, D (1999)*The Really Practical Guide to Primary English*. Cheltenham: Stanley Thornes.

Graham, J (1988) *Writing under Control*. London: David Fulton.

Graham, J (2000) *Reading under Control*. London: David Fulton.

Medwell, J (2002) *Primary English Knowledge and Understanding*. Exeter: Learning Matters.

National Literacy Strategy (1999) *Teaching and Learning Strategies*. London: HMSO.

Pollock, J (1999) *English Grammar and Teaching Strategies*. London: David Fulton.

Rose, A (1997) *Collins Grammar Rules*. London: Collins.

www.vtc.ngfl.gov.uk/resource/literacy/index.html This is the Virtual Teacher's Centre site which includes activities and examples of management of the Literacy Hour.

www.standards.dfee.gov.uk/literacy/activity Another government site with practical ideas.

www.ralic.rdg.ac.uk The Reading University Reading and Language Information Centre site.

www.acs.ucalgary.ca/~dkbrown/authors.html A site with information about a range of authors and links to publishers' pages, news about children's literature, reviews, lists etc. Canadian based.

www.scils.rutgers.edu/special/kay/kayhp2a.html This is a wonderful page with links to booklists, etc.

www.booktrust.org.uk/ybt.htm This is the site of Young Book Trust which holds copies of every children's book published in the UK in any year (6,000 titles). A source of information on books and authors.

http://www.literacytrust.org.uk A useful site.

3 MATHEMATICS

This chapter will:

→ discuss the changes in content and methods of teaching mathematics that may be familiar to you;

→ give you an outline of *what* you are currently expected to teach and *how* you are expected to teach mathematics in the primary school;

→ help you to identify issues that you may face, with practical suggestions to help you.

Background reading

To help you understand how mathematics is taught in primary schools you should gain access to copies of the following documents: *The National Curriculum: Mathematics Key Stages 1 and 2* (DfEE, 1999d) and *Curriculum Guidance for the Foundation Curriculum* (DfEE/QCA, 2000). Look at links to the National Numeracy Strategy (NNS, page 27) and mathematical development (pages 69–79). The section in grey below the 'stepping stones' relates to the key objectives in the NNS for the Reception year.

National Numeracy Strategy (DfEE, 1999e). Copies can be accessed via websites or ordered by telephone, fax or e-mail (details are given at the end of the book). Each section is clearly labelled. You may find it useful to turn to the examples for Year 6 in Section 6. This will give you a clear idea of the expectations for children by the end of primary school.

Also, try to obtain past Baseline Assessment and National Tests papers.

Background

When you hear about the NNS you may think there has just been a reversion to a traditional approach to teaching mathematics – class teaching. This is an easy assumption to make but not an accurate one. Mathematics has been taught in the primary school in a variety of ways during the last 30 or 40 years. A child-centred approach based upon Piaget's theories about how children learn was common in schools from the late 1960s and 1970s influenced by the Plowden Report (CACE, 1967).

Factors such as the end of selective education with the introduction of the comprehensive system, decimalisation of money in 1971 and industry changing to metric from imperial measures from 1975 gave greater scope for change in the curriculum. In primary schools published schemes (with an emphasis on understanding rather than rote learning) became commonplace. This was a time of children learning by discovery methods. Children were encouraged to take responsibility for their own learning.

However, this freedom within the curriculum came under increasing scrutiny. The Assessment of Performance Unit was launched in 1974 to monitor national standards at 11 and 15 years of age. In 1978 the Cockcroft Committee was set up. The wide-ranging report *Mathematics Counts* was published in 1982 (DES, 1982a). Amongst many other aspects of mathematics teaching it emphasised the importance of mental maths, whole-class teaching and the integration of problem-solving into the curriculum.

From the mid-1980s a number of reports were published – for example, the *International Assessment of Educational Progress* (IAEP, 1990). These reports showed that many of Cockcroft's objectives had been achieved. British children did well in applying maths to solve practical problems and were good in statistics and geometry but results were comparatively poor in numeracy. The White Paper published under the Conservative government, *Better Schools* (DES, 1982b), announced the intention to formulate national objectives. In 1987 a new Secretary of State, Keith Joseph, announced his intention to implement a national curriculum. In 1989 the National Curriculum was introduced with later revisions in 1991, 1995 and 2000. On 1 September 1992 the Office for Standards in Education (OFSTED) was set up with the aim of improving the standards and quality of education through inspection, public reporting and offering independent advice to schools.

Continuing concern about standards, fuelled by comparison with other countries, led to a number of projects being set up, the best known being the National Numeracy Project (NNP) in 1997. This advocated interactive, whole-class, direct teaching methods, mental maths, and the learning of number facts. Soon after the Labour government came to power in 1998, the White Paper *Excellence in Schools* was published, emphasising the raising of standards. Also in that year the NNS was launched. This took into account the approach of the National Literacy Strategy (NLS), in terms of pedagogy, as well as the NNP in terms of content and pedagogy. Although not compulsory, it is used in the majority of schools in England, and the revised National Curriculum (1999) reflects the thinking of the NNS. For the first time guidance was given (in the *Framework for Teaching Mathematics* – DfEE, 1999f) about the expectations teachers should have of the majority of children in a particular year group. The NNS established minimum standards, set out high expectations and announced the end of the so-called 'glass ceiling'. There was the politically driven expectation that the majority of children would succeed.

Some of the events and their effects may be familiar and part of your experience as a pupil, parent or teacher. They should give you a context and explanation of why we have reached the current stage in mathematics teaching.

Current practice

Statutory requirements

The National Curriculum has been the statutory requirement, giving an overview of mathematical content. The NNS framework did not change this requirement but set out this content in much more detail. No longer would schools need to write schemes of work to ensure coverage of the National Curriculum. The NNS framework is a comprehensive guide to the content and progression of the mathematics curriculum. It is divided into sections. Section 1 gives guidance on *how* to teach, while Section 3 contains planning grids. The subsequent sections identify key objectives, yearly teaching programmes and exemplary material for the key objectives. The content of the NNP related simply to numeracy; the NNS, however, includes all aspects of mathematics from the National Curriculem.

The content of the NNS is divided into five 'strands'.

1. Number and the number system.

2. Calculations.

3. Solving problems.

4. Measures, shape and space.

5. Handling data.

There is a clear correlation between the National Curriculum and the NNS. Prior to 1999, the NC included four Attainment Targets for mathematics.

1. Using and applying mathematics.

2. Number.

3. Shape, space and measures.

4. Handling data.

These are still retained but 'Using and applying mathematics' is incorporated into the other three Attainment Targets, and algebra has been included with number. The other 'strands' from the NNS can be easily identified in the 'new' NC. 'Number and the number system' and 'Calculations' are part of Attainment target 2 – 'Number and algebra'. It is also worth noting that the abbreviation for 'Attainment Target' (AT) has been changed simply to 'Ma' – which denotes that it relates to mathematics.

Although content has not changed greatly since the introduction of the NC in 1989, the emphasis has changed. One of the major changes has been with calculation. Mental mathematics now has prominence in each lesson. The strategies that children use for mental maths form the basis for more formal calculation skills. As a result of this emphasis, there have been other changes in content.

- Vertical calculations are no longer taught in Key Stage 1. This encourages the use of mental methods rather than standard algorithms.

- The use of calculators is no longer encouraged until Years 5 and 6, so children become secure in mental methods of calculation and do not become dependent on calculators.

- There is a change in the use of resources. The NNS advocates that, to calculate mentally, children have to become less reliant on structural apparatus (e.g. multi-link). Instead, resources that encourage children to form mental images of numbers and number systems are advocated. These include number lines, 100 squares, number cards and computer software.

Planning, assessment and differentiation

It could seem, from looking at the NNS framework, that a teacher has little part in deciding what to teach. However, the NNS stresses the importance of planning and assessment. In part, planning relates to *how* you will teach but also it is the means by which you match the subject content to the needs of the particular children in your class. To meet their needs you must assess. You may find that planning and assessment are far more formalised compared with your own school experiences. However, formats of planning grids are given to make the task easier. Planning needs to be based upon assessment. The NNS advocates class rather than individual assessment. For example, when reviewing the key objectives in the medium-term plan you could highlight what the majority of the children achieved and transfer objectives that have not yet been met on to the next plan. Detailed records would only be kept of children who had not met or who had exceeded expectations. 'Assess and review sessions' are written into the planning grids and to aid this process the NNS have now published supplementary guidance. As a result of assessment you would then be able to differentiate work to meet the needs of the pupils. The NNS recommends that teachers do not attempt to differentiate at more than three levels of difficulty so that it is manageable.

The NNS has now published unit plans and specimen lessons. The former emphasise what you will *teach* rather than what the children will *do*. The lesson plans are a guide but must be adapted by the teacher to meet the needs of the class. Also, there is now a set of materials called 'Springboard'. These are a series of lessons designed to provide additional support in booster classes for children who, with intensive targeted support, can achieve the expected National Tests levels (e.g. Level 4 in Year 6).

Structure of the Daily Mathematics Lesson

Both the NLS and the NNS emphasise the importance of structured lessons. This means having clear objectives that are shared with the class, whole-class oral work, direct interactive teaching and a summary at the end of the lesson called a 'plenary'. The format varies between the Literacy Hour and the Daily Mathematics Lesson.

The lesson is in three parts.

1. *Oral and mental starter* (5–10 minutes). Counting; practising mental calculations; recalling number, shape, space and measurement facts; deriving new facts from known facts; introducing or developing a mental strategy; using mental imagery; discussing the homework task. There is no requirement to link this part of the lesson to the main teaching part of the lesson. It can be used simply for revision.

2. *Main teaching and pupil activities* (30–40 minutes). Introducing a new topic; consolidating or extending previous work; using and applying concepts and skills; assessing children's learning.

3. *Plenary* (10–15 minutes). Informally assessing groups of children; clarifying misconceptions; reviewing objectives of the lesson; making connections with other maths work or other curriculum areas; setting homework task.

The lesson can last between 45 and 60 minutes depending largely on the age of the children. The organisation of the lesson should be flexible. As you can see, timing is not rigid as was originally advocated when the Literacy Hour was introduced into schools. Another feature of the Daily Mathematics Lesson that differs from the Literacy Hour is the way the time allocated. A teacher may feel that, if this were the first lesson of new work, the middle part of the lesson would be better spent working together as a class. Alternatively, there will be occasions when the teacher will minimise whole-class direct teaching and will want the children to work on activities in groups, pairs or individually. The important element to remember is that the teacher must try to ensure that he or she is *teaching* rather than *managing* all this time, whether it is to the whole class, a group, pair or individual.

Teaching methods

The first impressions of a maths lesson may confirm that much has been retained from former practice. Textbooks and work cards are frequently used, teachers use a board (although it tends to be white and not black) and chalk has been replaced by felt markers. However, it is the role of the teacher in teaching maths that has changed. A teacher cannot rely on a purely didactic approach to teaching, nor on a textbook and answer book giving both content and solution. No longer is mental maths from a book requiring children to write the answers down in silence and exchanging their books for marking with the child next to them, the teacher calling out the answers from the answer book. A teacher has to be proactive – has to have clearly defined objectives for a lesson that are then shared with the pupils. The lesson must be interactive. The teacher must *talk* to the children and respond to their *talk* with carefully considered questions and answers. Children are expected to articulate how they worked out answers. This requires the teacher to have a clear understanding of progression in mathematical concepts, an awareness of the sort of misconceptions children may form and an ability to avoid this happening or to put them right. He or she must consider the activities children will do that meet their ability but also take them forward in their learning. All this must be carried out in a lively, enjoyable way, maintaining a brisk pace so the children's interest is maintained. This may initially seem onerous but a great deal of guidance is given.

The NNS categorises this sort of teaching (which it calls 'direct teaching') under the following headings.

DIRECTING
At the beginning of the lesson or in part of the lesson, the teacher must help the children to understand **what** they are going to do or **how** they are going to set about a task:

Today we are going to find a way of adding fractions together.

Put the numbers you have found above each column.

INSTRUCTING
This means **breaking down** a task into stages which may include **giving a method** of doing something:

(Finding 75% of 16): first you must change the percentage into a fraction.

DEMONSTRATING
Demonstrating means **showing** (using apparatus or diagrams) how a mathematical idea can be understood or visualised:

(Using a number line 0–10): I am going to put $7\frac{1}{2}$ between the 7 and 8.

EXPLAINING AND ILLUSTRATING
This involves using **language** to communicate understanding or to relate mathematical idea to an example from **real life**:

(97 + 14): 97 is 3 less than 100 so I could add these two numbers together by adding 100 to 14 which is easy and then taking away 3.

Do you like pizza?

(Affirmative response.)

Which would you prefer – $\frac{1}{3}$ of a pizza or $\frac{1}{2}$ of a pizza?

QUESTIONING AND DISCUSSING
The teacher uses **language** in the form of questions or response to children's answers to take their understanding forward or to assess their understanding:

How could we subtract 97 from 114?

CONSOLIDATING
This means using **language** to find out what the children have learnt or discovered and **helping them to transfer their understanding** to a different context (e.g. **giving them homework**):

Can you explain how you knew that 9 was the answer?

When working with unit fractions): now we know that this number – the denomina-tor – tells us how many parts something has been divided into. If I show you these fractions ($\frac{1}{5}$ and $\frac{1}{10}$) can you tell me which is the larger fraction?

To practise what we have learnt today I would like you to go home and look for things in your house that are symmetrical. You can write them down or maybe draw them.

EVALUATING CHILDREN'S RESPONSES
This involves helping children discuss their mathematical ideas in a positive way:

Listen to John's idea and see if you think it would work.

Let's see what you think the answer is . . . we will write all the answers down and then think about them together.

SUMMARISING
The teacher uses language to help the children identify what they have learnt and tells them how it connects to other mathematical concepts or other areas of the curriculum. Tell them what they will be doing next:

Tell the rest of the class what you found out in your group today and maybe they could try your activity out at home.

Direct teaching requires children not just to understand but to use their increasing knowledge by applying it to further examples within the maths lesson and, if appro-priate, to other areas of the curriculum. This relies upon the teacher planning the whole curriculum carefully and making connections both within maths lessons and other curriculum subjects.

Preparing to teach

The following statements came from a group of teachers on a course for those returning to the profession. You may find they have similar thoughts to you:

I used to be happy about teaching maths and thought I did a good job but the way it's now taught has changed so much I have lost confidence.

I feel very uneasy about differentiation – I remember children having such varying ability that I can't see how they gain from been taught as a class. What about chil-dren with special needs or those who are gifted?

I'm used to unifix – I'm just not sure how to use these new resources even for something as straightforward as teaching number bonds.

I thought I was good at maths but there seems to be so much different terminology used today I don't know what teachers are talking about.

I have always lacked confidence in mathematics and struggled with it at school myself.

Such questions can be categorised under the following four headings.

1 Subject knowledge

Subject knowledge has frequently been identified as a problem (e.g. Cockcroft, 1982a), and this is borne out by recent research carried out by the Ontario Institute for Studies in Education about the NNS (DfES, 2001). It is a concern to many teachers. Unlike English (which is practised every day by reading, writing, speaking and listening), many aspects of maths are not used on a daily basis. However, good subject knowledge is important if a teacher is going to be effective. There are many ways you can improve your subject knowledge.

COURSES
In the long term you could investigate the possibility of going on a local authority course. These are usually only available as in-service provision (i.e. to those employed as teachers), but make enquiries to your local authority.

OBSERVATION
If a course is not possible and you are actively interested in returning to teaching, it may be possible for you to observe a leading mathematics teacher at work. Alternatively, arrange to go to a local school in a voluntary capacity. As well as supporting teachers you could ask to talk to the mathematics co-ordinator.

NNS TRAINING MATERIALS AND THE NNS FRAMEWORK
When the NNS was implemented a systematic programme of training was put in place. Ask if you can borrow some of the sources of information used for training that include written and video material. In the short term, use the *Framework* and work your way through the Year 5 and 6 examples. These are clearly set out and you may find they act as a reminder to you so that you are revising rather than learning something new.

Some people find that the standard written algorithms for addition, subtraction, multiplication and division are different from those they were taught. Again, use the examples in the *Framework* and supplement them with Key Stage 2 National Tests revision material that can be bought in most bookshops.

Questioning has been found to be a key to effective teaching and an area that has needed addressing since the NNS was implemented. There are exemplar questions in the QCA *Vocabulary* book (QCA, 1998) . There is also material on the Standards website.

THE INTERNET
The Internet provides a wealth of useful sites to support the teacher in subject knowledge. These sites range from identifying misconceptions to simply giving practical tips. However, the quality varies and the content is constantly changing. A list of potentially useful sites is given at the end of this chapter.

PREPARATION

Planning has already been identified as a key to teaching effectively. Writing a lesson plan may give you confidence both in subject knowledge and teaching methods when you go back into school. You need to consider the input *you* will make rather than just the activities the children will do. It is not so much the plan that is important but the process of writing the plan. It ensures that you have thought through every aspect of the lesson and so leave as little to chance as possible. You should also include questions you will ask and possible answers, explanations you will give and demonstrations you will use. This need not be used as a script. You can be more spontaneous but this will only come with increased levels of confidence you will acquire if you have plans you can rely on. Some teachers find this particularly useful with mental maths questions as it ensures that examples are carefully planned, strategies for calculation identified and, of course, the answers are available.

LITERATURE

Literature is a key source of information. You may find that literature written for initial teacher training is good for developing both subject and pedagogic knowledge and understanding (a list of suitable literature is included at the end of this chapter). Also, subscribe to magazines. *Primary Maths and Science* is published nine times a year and gives a wealth of practical ideas. *Mathematics in School* is the magazine of the Mathematical Association and this, again, gives many ideas for use in school.

2 Teaching methods

The introduction of the NLS and NNS has meant a significant change in the way children are taught these core subjects in the primary classroom. Depending when you last taught, the degree of change will vary. For example, information and communication technology (ICT) is an integral part of teaching. It is not just a subject in its own right but is taught across the curriculum. Apart from software programs that support children's learning of maths, use of ICT enables you to have access to a range of sources via the Internet (see details at the end of this chapter). There is also a range of other ICT resources that is used in the classroom, such as overhead projectors and overhead calculators. These help in the demonstrating mathematical ideas to a whole class. Increasingly, interactive whiteboards are being used in schools.

The focus on inclusive practice has also impacted significantly on teaching and learning. Research carried out for the government on the NNS by the Ontario Institute for Studies in Education (DfES, 2001) identified a concern over meeting the requirements of those identified as having special educational needs and providing sufficient challenge for those children who are mathematically gifted. The NNS has now published material to support teachers in these areas, and this is available on the Standards web pages (address at the end of the chapter).

OBSERVATION

Again, try to arrange to observe the teaching of mathematics. Keep focused observation notes. For example, the first time you observe, decide what you want to find out (e.g. questioning skills, how the teacher uses resources or the role of the teaching assistant). Just concentrate on recording that particular aspect of the lesson. Try to reflect on what you have learnt by summarising key ideas. If you are unable to observe a teacher, see if you can borrow NNS training material from a school (see above).

PRACTICE

When the NNS was introduced, teachers received training but their real learning came not from simulation via video or role play but by actually teaching the children in their class. So, once you have gained some confidence by observing, try to arrange with a school to 'have a go'. Have the confidence to ask the teacher to observe you and give you feedback. If you build up a rapport with a teacher and class from regular visits, this will not seem so daunting as you imagine.

PLANNING MEETINGS

Arrange to visit a school regularly and observe a planning meeting. If you are in a large school you will find that teachers frequently plan together. Increasingly, teaching assistants take part in planning meetings. Observing such meetings will help develop your knowledge and give you confidence in implementing the planning process.

3 Understanding terminology and the resources used

Every profession has its jargon. The jargon that you are familiar with may just have been replaced by a new version during the time you were out of the profession. When I first started teaching, set theory was the 'new' mathematics and everyday words like 'intersection' and 'universal' had specific mathematical meaning. Get a mathematics dictionary. This will help with some terminology. Words that come from everyday use, such as 'bridging to ten' and 'compensation' can be clarified by reading the *Framework*, where you can see the context in which the word or phrase is used. If in any doubt, check meaning with a practising teacher.

I started teaching using Dienes structural apparatus that was unfamiliar to me. Although such structural material is useful to show the relationship between numbers and partitioning of numbers, it is less frequently used today. However, there was a time when it was new to practising teachers. The resources used today are to help children develop mental images with less reliance on apparatus. It is thought that children learnt to manipulate apparatus without transferring their understanding to the number system. There are several strategies you can use so that you gain confidence with resources that are unfamiliar to you.

OBSERVATION

Observe a lesson and focus on the resources.

NNS VIDEOS

Watch a video. NNS videos identify the use of resources quite explicitly and give contexts for their appropriate use.

SOFTWARE

Play with equipment and computer software. Arrange a visit to a school or a local authority maths centre to view maths resources. In this way you will identify potential problems in their use (e.g. digit cards are best used on a table top rather than the carpet as they can easily be dropped). Number fans (digit cards secured together) are an adaptation of digit cards for use on the carpet.

CATALOGUES

Send for a catalogue. This will show you a range of resources, including computer software and may give you ideas for their use.

4 Change

Most people find it difficult to come to terms with change. For teachers practising during the changes that have taken place, it was a gradual process as the NNP was influential in changing practice before the NNS was officially introduced. Although many teachers felt that the strategies were imposed by government and that their professionalism was being undermined, they have, in the main, responded to them positively and the structure is evolving. This is partly in response to the views of practising teachers. Issues such as meeting the needs of the gifted child are being addressed by the strategy team, and information and guidance are constantly being published. It is too easy to condemn new practice from outside the profession. Make an active decision to try new methods and then make judgements.

Summary

- Changes in teaching mathematics involve both *what* to teach and *how* to teach it.

- The *Framework* gives detailed information on *what* to teach as well as some guidance on *how* to teach it.

- The DfES Standards website gives a wide range of information to support you in your teaching of mathematics.

- Don't be overwhelmed. Set yourself some short and long-term goals over a period of time. Mathematics is only one of the subjects you will teach. As a core subject it may be an important one that will be taught every day but that, in many senses, is an advantage as you will quickly gain experience teaching it. This in turn will give you confidence.

- Learn from other teachers. All teachers absorb or take ideas from their colleagues either consciously or unconsciously and use them directly or adapt them. Remember that the NNS was new to every primary teacher once.

Useful resources

Personal subject knowledge

Haylock, D (2001) *Mathematics Explained for Primary Teachers*. London: Sage.

Mooney, C, Briggs, M, Fletcher, M and McCullouch, J (2001) *Primary Mathematics: Teaching Theory and Practice*. Exeter: Learning Matters.

Mooney, C, Ferne, L, Fox, S, Hansen, A and Wrathmell, R (2000) *Primary Mathematics: Knowledge and Understanding*. Exeter: Learning Matters.

Suggate, J, Davis, A and Goulding, M (2001) *Mathematical Knowledge for Primary School Teachers*. London: David Fulton.

Pedagogic subject knowledge

DfEE (1999) *National Numeracy Strategy*. London: DfEE.

DfEE (1999) *Mathematics Vocabulary*. London: DfEE.

Headington, R (1997) *Supporting Numeracy*. London: David Fulton.

QCA (1999) *Teaching Mental Calculation Strategies*. London: QCA.

QCA (1999) *Standards in Mathematics: Exemplification of Key Learning Objectives from Reception to Year 6*. London: QCA.

Topping, K and Bamford, J (1998) *Parental Involvement and Peer Tutoring in Mathematics and Science*. London: David Fulton.

Topping, K and Bamford, J (1998) *The Paired Maths Handbook*. London: David Fulton.

www.ambleside.schoolzone.co.uk/ambleweb/numeracy.htm Excellent award-winning site recommended for ICT during the Numeracy Hour.

www.dfes.gov.uk/numeracy The National Numeracy Framework. Planning grids, teaching programmes and assessment activities. Advice on how to organise your lessons.

www.beam.co.uk/ Beam is a mathematics development project.

www.primaryresources.co.uk Ages 1 and 2. Materials for maths.

www.bbc.co.uk/learning/library/maths.shtml BBC maths site.

vtc.ngfl.gov.uk The Virtual Teacher's Centre.

nrich.maths.org.uk/index.html Mathematics enrichment.

www.education-quest.com *Primary Maths and Science Journal* website.

4 SCIENCE

This chapter will:

→ review the background to primary science teaching;

→ discuss the way that science is now taught in primary schools;

→ give an overview of ways that will help you to teach science well.

Background reading

To help you understand how science is currently taught in schools you will need copies of the following documentation: *The National Curriculum: Handbook for Primary Teachers in England* (DfEE, 1999b), *Curriculum Guidance for the Foundation Curriculum* (DfEE/QCA, 2000) and *Science: A Scheme of Work for Key Stages 1 and 2,* (QCA, 1998b). *Subject Report: Science* (OFSTED, 2002) – each year there is a review of their inspections. National Test (SATs) papers will give you an idea of the children's level at the end of primary school. There are reports on these National Tests that provide guidelines on teaching.

Background

When the idea of a National Curriculum was first being discussed, science was seen as a key part of a child's education. The influential HMI report, *Primary Education in England* (1978), identified a range of good practice in science. This good practice was often based on the major primary science projects of the 1960s and 1970s, such as Science 5–13 and Nuffield Junior Science. It also showed that many children were missing out on this key area of learning, modern life, the economy and the world of work. So, a range of initiatives was put in place to support teachers and schools in developing their science teaching. At that time primary science was generally seen to be a way of working, a way of understanding the world, rather than developing a knowledge and understanding of science ideas. The many publications of Science 5–13 give excellent support for teachers who wanted to develop their science teaching. One of the key publications was *With Objectives in Mind* (Ennever and Harlen, 1972). This saw the key aim of primary science teaching as *Developing an enquiring mind and a scientific approach to problem solving.* A key concern for the team was to help teachers be clear about their objectives. If the teacher knew what he or she wanted the children to learn they were more likely to learn it effectively. So the team published objectives to achieve this aim, grouped under a number of areas, such as:

- observing, exploring and ordering observations;

- developing basic concepts and logical thinking;

- posing questions and devising experiments or investigations to answer them.

These areas relate mainly to science as a way of working. By the time that the first draft of the National Curriculum was produced, research with children showed that the science ideas they had were often very different from the ideas that scientists had. This supported the move to have a greater focus on knowledge and understanding of key science ideas within the National Curriculum.

Current practice
Statutory requirements

In the 1999 version of the National Curriculum, the key parts of the Programme of Study for science are:

- Sc1 – scientific enquiry;

- Sc2 – life processes and living things;

- Sc3 – materials and their properties;

- Sc4 – physical processes;

- Breadth of study.

As you can see, the sections have a code and this often appears in school planning documents. So Sc1 is often used as an abbreviation for 'Scientific enquiry', Sc2 for 'Life processes and living things', and so on. The section 'Breadth of study' used to be at the beginning of the science section so it was often given the abbreviation Sc0. In the 1999 version of the Programme of Study it is at the end, but many schools still refer to it as Sc0.

For each of these sections there are a number of strands.

- *Sc1 – scientific enquiry* Ideas and evidence in science; and investigative skills (planning, obtaining and presenting evidence, considering evidence and evaluating).

- *Sc2 – life processes and living things* Life processes, humans and other animals, green plants, variation and classification, and living things and their environment.

- *Sc3 – materials and their properties* Grouping materials, changing materials and, in Key Stage (KS) 2, separating mixtures of materials.

- *Sc4 – physical processes* Electricity, forces and motion, light and, sound; and, in KS2, the earth and beyond.

Breadth of study has a section that relates to the contexts that we use for teaching science, and a section that relates to communication and to health and safety.

These strands are given for planning purposes to help focus our teaching. The beginning of the Programme of Study makes it clear that scientific enquiry should be taught through contexts taken from life processes and living things, materials and their properties, and from physical processes. Sometimes scientific enquiry will be the key focus of our teaching but it obviously has to be carried out within a scientific context. This linking is reinforced within 'Breadth of Study' where again it is made clear that knowledge skills and understanding should be taught using first-hand and secondary data to carry out a range of scientific investigations. We will see ways that we can do this in sections below.

Planning, assessing and differentiation

Most schools now use a two-year cycle for planning and teaching science. They cover each of the strands every two years. A common approach is to draw on the material in the Qualifications and Curriculum Authority (QCA) (1998b) scheme of work. Some schools adapt the material and suggested sequence to suit their own school and its context. Others draw on the QCA scheme material to teach their own long-term plans for science. This material is designed to fit into the typical allocation that schools make for teaching science. In the early years of schooling, pupils spend around one to one and a half hours on science. By the end of primary education the time given to science is more like one and a half to two hours a week. With the changes in the curriculum, especially in English and mathematics teaching, science is now usually taught to the whole class at the same time, rather than to groups at different times.

You should be able to see copies of the QCA scheme in school or on the website (the address is at the end of this book). As you would expect, each module gives the way it connects with previous work, the key vocabulary, resources and a range of expectations to show what pupils will have learnt by the end of the module. The modules specify what most children will have learnt, what would be the outcomes for children who have not made so much progress and what will be outcomes attained by children who have progressed further. By monitoring the children's science learning, you will be able to differentiate the tasks to meet their current attainment. For each module, there are specific objectives, suggested activities, links to other curriculum areas and points to note, including health and safety. Teachers with less experience in science teaching or returning to teaching worry about safety. This is an important consideration for us in teaching science and there is more about safety below.

Science is formally tested at the end of each key stage. At KS1, the teacher does the assessment. At the end of KS2, knowledge and understanding is assessed by National Tests and scientific enquiry is done by teacher assessment. The final statement of the level of attainment for each child is then taken from the levels from the assessment of scientific enquiry and of knowledge and understanding. This weighting again shows the importance of the two aspects of primary science.

Teaching scientific enquiry

Scientific enquiry is a key part of the National Curriculum. As we saw above, it is not something that can be taught free of some context in science knowledge and understanding. The history of primary science in the UK shows the strong tradition that there is for such an approach in primary science. The way that scientific enquiry contributes to the end of key stage assessment again reinforces this approach. What we also know is that where schools take an investigative approach to teaching and learning science, the pupils enjoy their science more, are more motivated to learn and are keener to carry on learning science. If we see that the role of schooling is to introduce pupils to learning for life, and learning for a career, this enthusiasm through an investigative approach is something we should foster. However, not all science can be taught through investigation. Work on aspects of human biology means we have to draw on a range of secondary sources, including books, models, video and games. In KS2, it is difficult to investigate aspects of work on the Earth in space. Some people suggest that it is also time consuming to work this way. However, the examples of good practice in HMI reports show that it is a better way to work and need not take more time. We can take a more flexible approach to timetabling, to give different-sized blocks of time to match the different purposes. We can sometimes have longer periods of time when we want our pupils to carry out a complete investigation, perhaps following the pupils' interests and ideas.

Perhaps the best known type of investigation is the fair test, something you may recognise from your previous experience. Here you help the pupils identify the key variables in an investigation, then they choose which one they will vary:

Pat, a teacher working with a reception class, was starting a topic on growing seeds. She asked the class 'What kinds of plants do you think grow from seeds?'. She got a range of responses from the pupils. Emma said 'green beans', Christopher thought 'sunflowers'. Jason suggested 'snapdragons' and Jessica thought 'cabbage.' Pat wrote the suggestion and the child's name on a sheet of paper as they said it. This gave a record of the pupils' starting points; it was something they could come back to at the end. The teacher then asked the children what they thought seeds need to help them grow and again Pat recorded the children's ideas. She recorded all their ideas to get them used to giving their ideas in class. Later in their schooling they would be expected to say why they thought theirs was a good idea and in Key Stage 2 they would be expected to challenge one another about their ideas.

Pat then talked to the children about what would make a difference to how the seeds would grow. She was introducing them to the idea of a variable. She asked them what might make a difference. She mostly led them to bipolar pairs of conditions that they might test. The conditions they came up with as ones they could test were:

soil – no soil
light – dark
water – no water – lots of water
hot – warm – cold
different growing materials (soil, sand, grass, stones, cotton wool).

They discussed the resources they would need and which groups would try which conditions. Badgers group decided to compare seeds in soil and seeds without soil. Tony thought 'The seeds in soil will grow. The seeds without soil will only grow a bit.' Chris thought 'The ones with soil will grow and the ones without soil won't grow'. Pat recorded their predictions. The seeds were monitored over the following days and the pupils' findings were recorded. In the Foxes group, Phil noticed 'The ones in the dark have grown long to try to get to the sun'. Jade said 'The green ones are healthier. The leaves are soft and flat and green. In the dark the leaves are yellow and all crumply.' These results and those of the other pupils were again recorded on sheets of paper with the child's name.

In this activity, the pupils were starting to give their ideas in science, they were identifying variables and starting to develop the notion of a fair test. The information was recorded as the children gave it and the sheets became a class *Bean Book*. This acted as a record of their work. They could compare their outcomes with their predictions. They saw the purpose of recording. They were proud of their book. Pat had a lot of information about the children's ideas and how they reported their findings. She could use these in her planning for their future work and as evidence for assessments. Later they would be able to see what type of variable they were working with:

- categoric variables – belonging to a class (e.g. seed type);

- discrete variables – ones that could have integer values (e.g. number of seeds);

- continuous variables – ones where there is an infinite number of possibilities (e.g. height of plant).

They would also learn in KS2 about the key variables in their investigation.

- *Independent variable* – the one the investigator chooses to change and how many values of this variable they should use.

- *Dependent variable* – the effect or the variable that changes as a result of changing the dependent variable, the one the investigator will measure or judge.

- *Control variables* – the variables the investigator keeps constant and how he or she will do that.

Pat's pupils were involved in structuring a complete investigation. However, we may not always have the time and resources available to follow the children's ideas. An alternative way is to allow the children control over part of their practical activity. You can use the strands of the Programme of Study (planning, obtaining and presenting evidence, and considering evidence and evaluating). The long-term planning for science will have identified the area to be taught and which aspects of enquiry will be given special attention. So where the focus within an activity is to be on planning we might allow the pupils to have control, or joint control with us, over one or more aspects of planning. So we can plan the following.

- Who will raise the question to be investigated?

- Who chooses the group of pupils to work in?

- Who selects of materials and tools ?

- Who selects the context for the investigation?

Suppose we were looking at insulation. We could look at this in the context of keeping drinks warm, on what to wear when we go to the beach, how to reduce our contribution to global warming, how to stop our ice cream melting on the way home from the shop. In principle, there is no reason why pupils should not decide which context to explore. From a scientific point of view there may not be much to choose between the contexts. From a classroom organisation or resourcing perspective some may well be easier to cope with than others. So we can decide whether to allow pupils to control the context, have joint control or no control. However, if the pupils never control their planning they are unlikely to learn to plan. As we saw with Pat's class, young children can be helped to make such decisions so there is no reason why older pupils should not be able to make similar decisions.

Once the context has been selected, we can see a range of ways that we can offer pupil control over the activity. It may be that we decide that we will structure the way the activity is carried out. This might be because of time constraints, resource constraints, safety concerns or a number of other options. Or we can offer the pupils some or all control over a range of aspects, the predictions, steps to be taken, timescale we working to, what form the results will take or how to decide that the activity is finished.

Similarly, as the children approach the end of the investigation, who will decide the audience for the results, the format for presenting the results? Who will compare the outcomes and the predictions, who will evaluate the investigation and what we have learnt as a result of carrying out the activity?

As we saw above, pupils like activities where they have some control over what happens. Pupils who like their work are more likely to learn from it. Letting them have control also improves their investigating. One of the key features of allowing control is that it helps make evident to the pupils why they are carrying out an activity. As you will know from earlier chapters, making clear the reason for the work we ask pupils to do helps them learn better. Helping them reflect on their learning helps improve understanding. It also contributes to their thinking skills and learning how to learn. Being clear about the lesson focus also helps us in our teaching. As we interact with pupils carrying out practical work, we can use the focus to help their learning. We can guide the pupils' observation to aspects they might not notice: 'Have you seen the way that . . .?' 'We can encourage them to move from the qualitative to the quantitative: 'How many . . .? How long . . .? How much longer do you think...? How often...? Do you think these are different?' And a partner to this one that pupils find more demanding: 'Do you think these are the same? What happens if you...? Can you make that one...?' These productive questions focus the children's investigating.

Most of the questions are person centred. The pupil is in the question – *you* see…, *you* make… Pupils tend to give longer, better responses when they are in the question. They see it as implying that their view counts. Thinking questions, ('Do you think…?') encourage the pupils to think, something at the heart of education. As teachers we ask thousands of questions a year. Making our questions better should have a powerful impact on our teaching. Dillon (1994) argues that we should also use other strategies like silence. If we have asked somebody to think we should give that person time to do it. In UK classrooms teachers typically wait about 0.6 seconds before they do something. It is very difficult to think as opposed to recall in that time. If we want pupils to think we should give them time to do it. Try waiting for 2, 3 or 4 seconds for a reply. That gives the pupils time to think and frame their response. It also gives us, as teachers, time to think of a better question if the pupils don't answer us. Similarly, after the pupil has spoken, teachers wait about 0.4 seconds. If we increase that wait time to 2 or 3 seconds, we are again more likely to get a better response, or a response from another pupil. Increasing wait-time is one of the best ways to improve learning. I also know that it is a very tricky thing to do as we are so schooled into thinking we have to keep the lesson moving along.

Teaching scientific knowledge and understanding

There are three major changes to teaching knowledge and understanding that have taken place during the life of the National Curriculum. The first change is that teachers have realised that children have well developed ideas about many science concepts though these may not agree with scientists' ideas. Most of us can think of children giving cute or odd responses to our questions. We now realise that these responses tell us much about children's thinking. If we listen to what they say, we can build on their ideas to help their science learning.

The first time I realised the importance of this was when I had asked a group of Year 1 children to sort a set of everyday materials into two sets: a solids set and a liquids set. Kas had put the table salt and the icing sugar in with the liquids:

> Kas argued, 'Look, you can put your finger in it. And you can pour it from one pot to another. Look. See?'

> I asked, 'Does it go level in the pot when you pour it?'

> 'Sort of. Look it goes to the shape of the pot. It's like a water drop on top. Nearly flat.'

It was then that I thought Kas was right. The argument is perfectly logical, showing how the observations and the conclusions fit. By the next time we had science, I had thought of using different types of salt, coarse sea salt, cooking salt and table salt. I asked them whether they thought the sea salt was solid or liquid. They said they were small solid bits. I asked them how they could make the bits of salt smaller. So they set to grind up the sea salt till it was fine and they could pour it like the table salt they had used last time. They now realised that the table salt was made of small solid pieces, which seemed to behave like a liquid but when you look carefully, you can see they are solid. This taught me the value of listening carefully to what they had to say as a way to make my science teaching better. The pupils learnt an important scientific idea from it. They also learnt something about checking our ideas in different circumstances to see how well they fit – again another important aspect of science learning.

The second change in teaching science knowledge and understanding is to help the pupils be clear about our purpose. If they have been involved in planning the science activity, they are more likely to see the purpose. The 'Breadth of study' helps us to make this explicit, as we define the context for the science work.

The third change is helping pupils make connections between their ideas. We can also explain how the current work fits with previous work and also with work that will happen later. Recent schemes, such as the QCA scheme, tell the teacher how the scheme planned for these links. We can help the pupils' learning by making these links explicit to the pupils too. As in mathematics and literacy lessons, this linking is one of the key aspects of the plenary session where we help the pupils review their learning, show them new links and how it will connect to future work.

Health and safety

We all have images, from school, from the media such as film and television, of science as a dangerous activity. It certainly can be. However, the sorts of activities recommended for primary science are generally very safe and usually use knowledge that most people have, rather than specialist knowledge. The Association for Science Education have produced a small book, *Be Safe!* (ASE, 2001), which shows the range of safety issues in each of the main topics in primary science. It tells you what to avoid, what is safe and what precautions to take if there is a risk associated with an activity. They show how to do a risk assessment for a science activity.

Most of the hazards are obvious, such as cuts from sharp or broken equipment. Very few are less obvious. One that has been the focus of attention is the risks associated with investigating change. If foodstuffs are used as samples of what happens when things change, then a range of growths can appear. Penicillin mould often appears on bread, for instance. You probably know that a small proportion of people have a powerful allergic reaction to penicillin, so contact with such mould should be avoided. This is easily done by having the samples of foodstuffs in sealed, transparent containers. The children can see what is going on without being able to breathe in the moulds. The container can then be disposed off at the end of the activity without opening it.

Preparing to teach science
Subject knowledge

Many people have a less positive view of their own secondary school science. Yet surveys show that people are keen to know about topics to do with their health, the environment and new ways of doing things. This means you will have acquired a lot of science knowledge informally to add to that you learnt formally. There is a wide range of books available to support teachers of primary science. There is a wealth of material available on the Internet (see the end of this chapter for details). However, for most of us when we teach science there are often pupil questions we cannot answer. You're not the first person, and I hope you won't be the last person, to be in this situation. You can try turning the question round into a form that can be investigated. Wynne Harlen (1985) suggests this format.

Analyse the question

↓

Consider if it can be 'turned' to practical activity (with its 'real' materials or by simulating them)

↓

Carry out a 'variables scan' and identify productive questions

↓

Use questions to promote activity

↓

Consider simple generalisations children might make *from experience*

If you need help with everyday science, try **www.newscientist.com/lastword/**. Here there are answers to questions such as: 'Why does the first person with a new packet of breakfast cereal always get the best bits?'

Finding out children's ideas

This is an important aspect of teachers' work. You could try one of the following approaches with a small group of children. In recent years, a number of projects have worked on children's ideas in science and what we can do about them. The Nuffield Primary Science project has produced a set of teacher and pupil materials which have a wide range of ideas for helping pupils develop their science knowledge and understanding. If you read one of their teacher's books designed for the age range you will teach, you can see how they suggest we identify children's starting points, what we do with these ideas, how to cope with the different children's ideas and what the implications are for organising and monitoring children's learning.

A recent development has been the use of 'concept cartoons' to help children express their views. Figure 4.1 shows such a cartoon. The cartoon shows a situation with some children's views about it. The class decides in small groups which person they agree with in the cartoon. The argument is that it is easier to debate views already given than clarify your own. It is also easier to talk about the ideas of some other child rather than your own or the teacher's ideas. Further examples are available in book form and on the Internet (details are given at the end of this chapter).

Figure 4.1 A concept cartoon

Yet another way to help children make their ideas clear is to ask them to write about them or to draw them. Figure 4.2 gives an example from the start of a topic by Anna, a Year 5 child writing and drawing about what happens to food when we eat it. One way to look at this is to say she has a very confused notion about digestion. A more positive way is to see that Anna has a lot of knowledge about digestion and her body. My role as a teacher is to build on, and refine, these ideas to help Anna make connections between these various pieces of information. That will make it easier to show her how the scientists' ideas fit her knowledge and give her a more powerful framework to understand this topic.

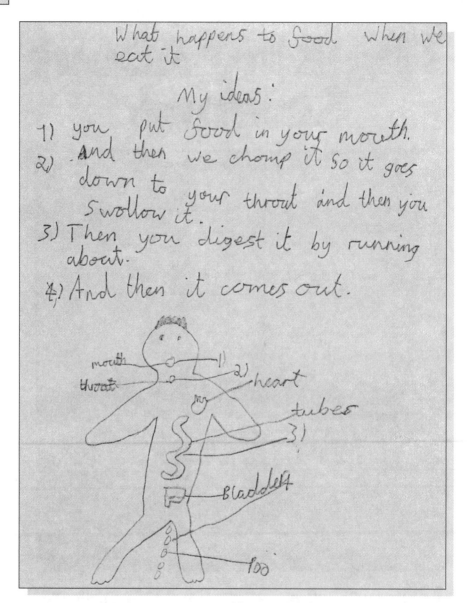

What happens to food when we eat it

My ideas:
1) you put food in your mouth.
2) And then we chomp it so it goes down to your throat and then you swollow it.
3) Then you digest it by running about.
4) And then it comes out.

mouth
throat
heart
tubes
3)
Bladder
Poo

Figure 4.2 What happens to food when you eat it

Questioning

The importance of question types and of wait-time has been stated above. Try to work with a group of pupils and to record your discussion. You will need permission from the school to make such a recording, but as long as it is for your own purposes this is normally not a difficulty. Practise increasing your wait-time. At first I found it very uncomfortable. So now I count out the seconds to measure my wait-time. Try asking thinking questions, open questions and closed questions to see how you and your pupils respond. Do not be upset if you do not match your ideals. We have spent years acquiring one way of teaching. It may take years to become proficient at another way of working.

Summary

- Primary science is one area where teachers and schools are doing a very good job.

- It is an area children enjoy.

- The constant ingenuity of pupils in interpreting their world provides endless fascination and challenge for the teacher and the other pupils.

- Science is an area where teachers seem to be able to draw on their own knowledge and their good practice to achieve real learning for the pupils, for themselves and the satisfaction of a job well done.

- Teachers can improve their pupils' science learning and investigating by asking productive, person-centred questions.

- Finding out our pupils' ideas is a valuable resource for supporting pupil learning.

- If you leave time for your pupils to think about and answer your science questions, their thinking and learning improves.

Useful resources

Books to develop your subject knowledge

Devereaux, J (2000) *Primary Science*. London: Paul Chapman.
Farrow, S (1999) *The Really Useful Science Book* (2nd edn). London: Falmer Press.
Nuffield Primary Science (1997) *Understanding Science Ideas: A Guide for Primary Teachers*. London: Collins Educational.

Books on teaching science

Harlen, W (1985) *Taking the Plunge*. London: Heinemann (very good on teacher and pupil questions).
Harlen, W (2000) *The Teaching of Science in Primary Schools* (3rd edn). London: Paul Chapman.
Naylor, S and Keogh, B (2000) *Concept Cartoons in Science Education*. Sandbach: Millgate House Publishers.

For help with teaching investigating

Goldsworthy, A (1999) *Teach it! Do it! Let's get to it! How Direct Teaching of Science Skills Helps Children to Investigate (5–11 years)*. Hatfield: Association for Science Education.
Goldsworthy, A and Feasey, R (1997) *Making Sense of Primary Science Investigations*. Hatfield: Association for Science Education.

Safety in science

ASE (2001) *Be Safe! Health and Safety in Primary School Science and Technology* (3rd edn). Hatfield: Association for Science Education.

ICT and science

Roger Frost's dataloggerama: **www.rogerfrost.com/**

Help with knowledge and understanding about science

There is self-directed study, such as

www.le.ac.uk/education/centres/sci/selfstudy.htm

You could try 'Ask a teacher' at the BBC site **www.bbc.co.uk/education/ gcsebitesize/** or at Channel 4 **www.4learning.co.uk/apps/homework/science/** Dr Universe, a clever female cat, runs a website at **www.wsu.edu/druniverse/** which is appreciated by children.

At **www.sciencenet.org.uk** they have a list of previous science questions, with answers. You can leave your question and they will email you an answer, though it can take a few days. Or you can ring them on 0808 800 4000 between 1 p.m. and 7 p.m. Monday to Saturday.

Other useful websites

The Association for Science Education **www.ase.org.uk** – many links from this site. Natural History Museum Quest site **www.nhm.ac.uk/education/quest2/ englisg/index.html** The Science Museum site **www.nmsi.ac.uk**

This chapter will:

→ identify the changes in this area of the curriculum since the introduction of the National Curriculum in 1988;

→ show how the non-core foundation subjects interrelate in the school curriculum;

→ prepare you to teach across the whole curriculum.

Background reading

To help you understand the statutory requirements of non-core foundation subjects within the National Curriculum, you will need to look at the following documentation: *The National Curriculum: Handbook for Primary Teachers in England* (DfEE, 1999b), *The Curriculum Guidance for the Foundation Stage* (QCA, 2000) and *Designing and Timetabling the Primary Curriculum – a Practical Guide for Key Stages 1 and 2* (QCA, 2002).

You may also find it useful to read the Office for Standards in Education (OFSTED) subject reports for primary phase available in hard copy or on the OFSTED website **http://www.ofsted.gov.uk/public/index.htm**

Background

Some of you will remember a time before the introduction of the National Curriculum when the content of the curriculum was totally determined at a local level. Class teachers and subject co-ordinators devised schemes of work and support was given by the local education authority (LEA) in the form of courses and advisory teams for each subject. It was a time when the curriculum was frequently organised using a thematic approach. A topic such as 'North American Indians' would lead interrelated subject content. Figure 5.1 gives an example of how this theme might have been organised.

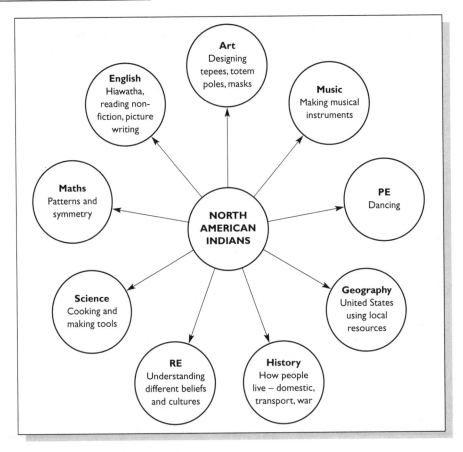

Figure 5.1 A thematic approach

As well as identifying subject areas, connections were made across subjects. For example, music would be linked to dancing that would in turn be linked to English in the form of dramatising Hiawatha's wedding. These links made the diagram look like a spider's web—hence the term 'topic web'. Although advocated in the Plowden Report (CACE, 1967) this holistic approach to learning and teaching was criticised for generality and lack of progression in developing basic skills. Learning about the world was thought to be best if it was organised through systems of thinking and teaching that subjects represented. However, at its best it gave the teacher scope to be imaginative in developing the curriculum and could relate to children's interests. The topic approach did not disappear in 1988 with the introduction of the National Curriculum but it became much less prevalent in schools because of the National Curriculum's subject-orientated focus.

Since then, the National Curriculum has undergone many changes in scope and emphasis. Initially it was criticised for its prescriptive nature and assessment procedures. Although time was meant to be available within the curriculum to respond to individual and local interests, this rarely happened as the original National Curriculum was so overloaded. Also the fact that the curriculum was subject based (each written by subject experts) meant important elements of the curriculum were excluded, such as personal, social and health education. In response to the latter criticism, schools were advised in 1990 to adopt five cross-curricular themes.

- Economic and industrial understanding.

- Health education.

- Education for citizenship.

- Environmental education.

- Careers education (for secondary education).

Sex education was added to compulsory requirements in 1993 and, in 1994, OFSTED published a paper on spiritual, moral, social and cultural development. But it was the review conducted by Sir Ron Dearing in 1994–95 that changed the National Curriculum significantly by advising a more manageable curriculum and a reduction in the number of attainment targets.

In 1998–99, the introduction of the National Literacy and Numeracy Strategies led to a marginalisation of subjects other than English and mathematics. Not only did this affect non-core foundation subjects but also science (the other core subject), and many schools found it increasingly difficult to meet statutory obligations.

In 1998, the government issued interim arrangements to run for a period of two years. The requirements to follow the full Programmes of Study were relaxed in most of the non-core foundation subjects. Swimming remained statutory as did the requirements for English, mathematics, science and information and communication technology. The Qualifications and Curriculum Authority (QCA) offered guidance on how to teach core and foundation subjects in a document called *Maintaining Breadth and Balance at Key Stages 1 and 2* (QCA, 1999). It was suggested that schools prioritised, combined or reduced the non-core foundation subjects, essentially effecting a narrowing of the curriculum. For example, in a unit of work about Victorian Britain, schools could chose a focus such as 'children'. Some schools followed this guidance while others endeavoured to maintain a broad curriculum.

To counter criticisms that the curriculum had become too narrow, the government set up a number of advisory bodies to advise on the curriculum, including the National Advisory Committee on Creative and Cultural Education (NACCCE). NACCCE published the report, *All Our Futures: Creativity, Culture and Education*, in May 1999 which stated that a national strategy for creative and cultural education is necessary if all children are to develop their potential and so contribute to society, and which offered guidance to a range of organisations including government, schools and LEAs. The revised National Curriculum, issued in 2000, reflects, to some degree, the view expressed by NACCCE (and other similar advisory bodies).

Current practice

From September 2000, primary schools once again have to follow all the requirements of the revised National Curriculum in the non-core foundation subjects. However, these requirements are less prescriptive than formerly to enable a continued emphasis on literacy and numeracy.

In Key Stages 1 and 2, there are seven statutory non-core foundation subjects.

1. Design and technology (D&T).

2. Information and communication technology (ICT).

3. History.

4. Geography.

5. Art and design.

6. Music.

7. Physical education (PE).

Schools should aim to provide two hours of physical activity including extra-curricular activities. At Key Stage 2, swimming is a compulsory part of the curriculum.

Depending on when you last taught, the titles of some subjects may look different. Art has now become 'art and design' *to reflect the breadth of the subject and its contribution to the design and creative industries* (QCA, 1999). The term 'technology' appears both in 'design and technology' and in 'information and communication technology'. In the latter it is taught both as a subject in its own right and as an integral part of other subjects across the curriculum. The speed with which technology has become part of our lives means that children now need knowledge, skills and understanding that are far beyond what was thought necessary 15 years ago.

Additional requirements

In the National Curriculum (1999), advice is given on the following.

RELIGIOUS EDUCATION (RE)
All primary schools must provide religious education but the subject is not compulsory for all pupils since parents may withdraw their children from these lessons if they wish. Religious education is not classed as a foundation subject. State and church-controlled schools use locally agreed syllabuses or QCA schemes but church-aided schools usually follow a diocesan syllabus.

SEX EDUCATION
In Key Stages 1 and 2 schools must have a policy on sex education. If sex education is provided, parents may withdraw their children from the lessons.

PERSONAL, SOCIAL AND HEALTH EDUCATION (PSHE) AND CITIZENSHIP
Guidance is given to schools on PSHE and citizenship but it is not part of the National Curriculum. Citizenship became statutory from August 2002 for Key Stages 3 and 4.

MODERN FOREIGN LANGUAGES (MFL)
A modern foreign language may be taught in Years 5 and 6 of Key Stage 2 and guidance is given in the National Curriculum. Foreign languages are only statutory from Key Stage 3.

DRAMA

Drama is an integral part of English. However, some schools see it as an important aspect of the school curriculum and provide an additional range of opportunities for children to participate in the subject from school plays to drama clubs. Some drama will feature as part of the English curriculum in all schools.

KEY SKILLS

Key Skills are generic skills that have been identified as necessary for work and life-long learning. They are:

- communication;

- application of number;

- information technology;

- working with others;

- improving own learning and performance;

- problem-solving.

It is not expected that Key Skills will be taught separately but rather that opportunities for their development are identified in planning.

THINKING SKILLS

Thinking skills include the following.

- Information-processing skills.

- Reasoning skills.

- Enquiry skills.

- Creative thinking skills.

- Evaluation skills.

Again, it is expected that these skills will be integrated into subject teaching so children have opportunities to develop them.

PROMOTING SPIRITUAL, MORAL, SOCIAL AND CULTURAL DEVELOPMENT

Explicit opportunities for promoting this development within the curriculum can be found in RE and PSHE and citizenship. It's also possible to promote spiritual, moral, social and cultural development in school behaviour management policies (see Chapter 7).

QCA schemes of work and unit plans

Many schools now follow schemes of work published by the QCA. Some use them directly whilst others adapt them considerably to meet the needs of their individual school and children. They can be found electronically on the QCA website (see the end of this book) or obtained directly from the QCA.

The Foundation stage

The Foundation stage should not be confused with the non-core foundation subjects. The Foundation stage begins when children reach the age of three. The government became actively involved in nursery education when it provided funding in the form of vouchers to parents to be used to pay for education for children below statutory school age. With funding provision came requirements for education provision. These were published as Desirable Learning Outcomes in 1998. A consultation on the Desirable Learning Outcomes and proposals for curriculum guidance for a distinct stage of education from three to the end of the Reception year was carried out and a report published in June 1998. In October 1999 the Early Learning Goals were published. These are very similar to the Desirable Learning Outcomes. Further guidance followed in May 2000 when the document *The Curriculum Guidance for the Foundation Stage* was published (QCA, 2000). It gives guidance on six areas of learning.

1. Personal, social and emotional development.

2. Communication, language and literacy.

3. Mathematical development.

4. Knowledge and understanding of the world.

5. Physical development.

6. Creative development.

The Early Learning Goals in communication, language, and literacy and mathematical development link directly to the teaching objectives in the frameworks for teaching literacy and mathematics in the Reception year.

Whether you are going to teach in the Foundation stage or not, it is useful to see how the Early Learning Goals relate to the National Curriculum.

Cross-curricular work

The National Curriculum suggests links to other curriculum areas (see text in the margin in grey font) as well as emphasising the importance of making links to language and ICT. Pressure on the timetable to accommodate the literacy and numeracy strategies means that some schools are using a topic-work approach with a single or multi-subject focus in order to meet all the statutory requirements. Topic, or thematic, work has been the subject of much criticism (most recently from OFSTED) because it can lead to lack of teaching focus and progression. However, if well planned and linked not just to the acquisition of knowledge but also to skills, it can be a pragmatic way to manage coverage of the full curriculum. OFSTED (2002) acknowledged that 'imaginative' ways to timetable the curriculum were having growing success. New guidance has now been published by the QCA (2002) for teachers to use in the academic year 2002–2003 which focuses on flexibility in the design and timetabling of the curriculum while meeting the statutory requirements. Examples of practice in schools have been included in this guidance.

Assessment

National Tests are used to assess core knowledge and understanding in English and mathematics at Key Stage 1 and English, mathematics and science at Key Stage 2. Teachers report to parents on the non-core foundation subjects in general terms but not by level, but an OFSTED inspection would comment on children's progress and expect to see evidence of assessment in relation to the levels identified in the National Curriculum. Each year OFSTED publishes subject reports on their findings. OFSTED inspectors specialise in a number of foundation subjects and assess performance by looking at documentation, reviewing work, talking to children and watching lessons. (For further information on assessment, see Chapter 6.)

Current issues

The curriculum in any school is made up of formal, informal and hidden aspects. The formal curriculum is the legally required curriculum identified above. What makes schools different and so influences where a parent chooses to send his or her child is the informal curriculum. This covers factors such as what happens at playtime and in after-school clubs. The hidden curriculum relates to the ethos of the school (see Chapter 7 for more information). All these aspects of the curriculum make the school unique.

The non-core foundation subjects need to be seen within the context of the whole school curriculum. School plays, sports days and charity events all interrelate with the whole curriculum. The way a school addresses curriculum issues is an important indicator of the philosophy of the school.

The status of non-core subjects has diminished since the introduction of a National Curriculum and there is growing concern over the diminishing quality of work in non-core foundation subjects. Colin Richards (2000), using a football analogy, sums up recent trends as follows:

> The members of the 'first division' are English, maths and science (the latter always dangerously near to relegation); in the 'second division', are the subjects of history, geography and technology, the 'third division' subjects are art, music and physical education, while cross curricular themes are part of 'non-league' provision.

> Richards, 2000, p. 32.

OFSTED has recently warned of *a serious narrowing of the primary curriculum*. At the time of writing, the result is a review of the curriculum chaired by Baroness Ashton to be reported on in 2005.

Preparing to teach
Subject co-ordinators/leaders

The role of subject leaders is to provide the leadership, subject expertise and enthusiasm that teachers need to understand and implement the various elements of the curriculum. Usually, each subject is the responsibility of a designated teacher although, in small schools, a teacher may be responsible for two or more subjects.

During your school experience, you should choose an aspect of the curriculum in which you have expertise or an interest as a starting point to find out how the curriculum is organised. For example, if you have an interest in PE you could identify the documentation relating to PE, how planning takes place, links with local authorities, courses and the range of opportunities for PE in the curriculum including after-school clubs and staffing of PE. Other aspects to consider are resources, approaches to teaching and learning, the role of school visits and how assessments relate to portfolios of children's work.

Planning

LONG TERM

Looking at the school's long-term planning will help you identify how the school has identified progression in each key stage for each subject. If detail is limited to subject content (e.g. 'Second World War'), you may have to ask the subject co-ordinator, in this example it would be the history co-ordinator, questions about more detail on how this is covered in relation to other curriculum areas and the development of skills. It is also useful to ask whether QCA plans are used and, if so, to what extent they are modified. Check how time is allocated to subjects, particularly between core and foundation. Is there a system of double counting or not?

MEDIUM TERM

The class or year group, medium-term planning should give you more detail on content coverage and how one subject relates to another (many medium-term plans identify cross-curricular links). Skills learnt in the Daily Mathematics Lesson and Literacy Hour could be practised in other subject areas. For example, children could distinguish between fact and fiction in history, detect bias in geography and use setting in historical fiction. It is quite common to find that a subject specialist does the planning for teachers in the foundation subjects across the school. The teacher will simply adapt those plans to meet the needs of the children in the class.

Planning documents should also show you how cross-curricular requirements such as PSHE are addressed and tracked. They may give you insight into school policies and how children learn, including the role of play, displays and drama in children's learning.

SHORT TERM

It is up to the individual teacher to plan each lesson for his or her class. Be specific about what you are trying to teach and how you will know if you have been successful. You need to bring about learning (i.e. teach) rather than just facilitate learning. This means that you must be secure in your subject knowledge.

Summary

It is beyond the scope of this book to consider every aspect of teaching foundation subjects in primary schools but the important points for you to consider are as follows.

- The changing emphasis of the role of the non-core foundation subjects in education since the introduction of the National Curriculum.

- The National Curriculum should be seen as only part of the school curriculum.

- Non-core foundation subjects should be seen in the context of the whole curriculum, and cross-curricular links made *between* subjects as well as with the additional requirements of the National Curriculum (such as PSHE) in order to cover the full curriculum.

- Revisions to the National Curriculum, and to the place of the foundation subjects within it, are currently being planned.

Useful resources

Ashley, M and Hughes, M (1999) Towards uncertain futures?, in Ashley, M (ed) *Improving Teaching and Learning in the Humanities*. London: Falmer Press.

Craft, A (2000) *Creativity across the Primary School*. London: Routledge.

Jackson, E (2000) Citizenship, in Grimwade, K et al. (eds) *Geography and the New Agenda: Citizenship, PSHE and Sustainable Development in the Primary Curriculum*. Sheffield: Geographical Association.

Johnston, J, Chater, M and Bell, D (2002) *Teaching the Primary Curriculum*. Milton Keynes: Open University Press.

NACCCE (1999) *All our Futures: Creativity, Culture and Education*. London: DfES.

Sharp, J, Potter, J, Allen, J and Loveless, A (2002) *Primary ICT: Knowledge, Understanding and Practice* (2nd edn). Exeter: Learning Matters.

Designing and Timetabling the Primary Curriculum – A Practical Guide for Key Stages 1 and 2 (order code QCA/02/912) can be found at **www.qca.org.uk/ca/5-14/learning_prim_curr.asp**. Copies have been sent to all primary schools. Further copies can be ordered from QCA Publications on 01787 884444.

This chapter will:

→ identify recent changes in assessment;

→ review current approaches to assessment;

→ provide guidance on how to assess with examples of possible formats for assessing and recording.

Background reading

It is recommended you read the following documentation: *The National Curriculum: Handbook for Primary Teachers in England* (DfEE, 1996b). Select a core and foundation subject and study the Levels of Attainment. *Curriculum Guidance for the Foundation Stage* (DfEE/QCA, 2000). Identify the Early Learning Goals for communication, language and literacy, and mathematical development on pages 44–81.

As a returner, you should thoroughly familiarise yourself with National Tests in English, mathematics and science including the teachers' handbooks, Office for Standards in Education (OFSTED) data and the annual Qualifications and Curriculum Authority (QCA) assessment reports.

Background

Some of you may remember a time, prior to the introduction of the National Curriculum, when there was no national testing in primary schools. Many local education authorities (LEAs) had abandoned the 11+ examinations as secondary schools had become fully comprehensive. Most LEAs required their schools to use locally chosen tests in English (mainly of reading) and mathematics to assess children's attainment and progress. Schools and teachers would also use published tests and developmental measures in order to assess children for grouping, setting and sometimes streaming. Consequently, expectations and practice varied considerable between schools and authorities.

The first National Curriculum was introduced in 1988 and combined formative and summative approaches to assessment. Formative assessment provides information which teachers can use to decide how a pupil's learning should be taken forward. Summative assessment provides overall evidence of achievements. The National Curriculum gave eight levels through which children progressed from the age of five to the end of compulsory education at 16 and the expectation was that the average child would attain his or her expected level for his or her chronological age. At the end of Key Stage 1 most children were expected to gain Level 2 in all subjects and at Key Stage 2 Level 4 was expected.

Assessments of the core subjects were carried out by teachers in two ways.

1. Collecting and appraising samples of children's work.

2. Administering nationally set tasks which were integrated into the existing timetable.

That this method was unwieldy and time-consuming was eventually acknowledged by the government and the tasks were replaced by pen-and-paper National Tests (commonly called SATs). At Key Stage 1, children do National Tests in English and mathematics and at Key Stage 2 they do National Tests in English, mathematics and science.

Increasingly, and particularly after the advent of OFSTED, schools feel under pressure to improve their National Test results. It is common to find school improvement plans being based around OFSTED reports targeting specific areas for attention, and the publication of league tables at Key Stage 2 (based on National Test results) has put further pressure on schools to improve their performance. It could be said that there is a new culture within schools emphasising improvement of children's attainment and teacher accountability – affecting teaching career progression and offering value for money.

The focus on assessment has prompted several pieces of research, notably that by Black and Wiliam (*Inside the Black Box*, 1998b). This points to increasingly strong evidence that formative rather than summative assessment raises standards. Recently, formative assessment has become known as 'assessment for learning'. QCA (1999b) has acknowledged that effective assessment for learning is a key factor in raising standards.

The characteristics of assessment that promotes learning are that it:

- is embedded in a view of teaching and learning of which it is an essential part;
- involves sharing learning goals with pupils;
- aims to help pupils to know and to recognise the standards they are aiming for;
- involves pupils in self-assessment;
- provides feedback which leads to pupils recognising their next steps and how to take them;
- is underpinned by confidence that every student can improve;
- involves both teacher and pupils reviewing and reflecting on assessment data.

Current practice

At the beginning of the school year teachers are likely to receive information on the achievements of their new class, expressed as National Curriculum levels (possibly with additional finer grading of c = 'just the level', b = 'mid-level' and a = 'secure at level') in reading, writing, spelling, mathematics and, sometimes, in science. Teachers are expected to indicate the target levels to be reached by the end of the year and to use the information to plan for differentiation. You may well be handed a list of numerical targets for reading, writing and mathematics which you will be expected to meet by the end of the year. The targets will be part of the school's drive to reach targets set by the head teacher and governors, and will have been approved by the LEA.

From September 1998 all children were assessed when they first started school. For most children this was when they joined a Reception class at age of four or five. It was called 'Baseline Assessment' and was carried out within the first half-term of the child starting school. There were many Baseline Assessment schemes but all had to be approved by the QCA. From September 2002, it is replaced by the Foundation Stage Profile which should be finalised by June, each year, as part of an 'end of Foundation stage assessment' to assist teachers in planning for progression in Year 1 as children start Key Stage 1.

Teachers also receive Individual Educational Plans (IEPs) from the co-ordinator for special educational needs so that they can ensure that the progress of individual children is monitored regularly and targets and support are adjusted accordingly.

When you start teaching a new class, it can be useful to look at test scripts for selected children or groups of children. For example, a review of the scripts for children gaining 2b on mathematics at the end of Year 2 can highlight patterns in the questions not attempted, those tried but answered incorrectly and the range of strategies used to solve problems. This can give insights into the needs of children who are broadly '2b' but not yet '2a' and, when translated into curriculum content and teaching approaches in mathematics, can assist planning, teaching and target-setting.

Most schemes of work, or 'medium-term plans', include details of assessment. Teachers assess in many ways (e.g. through observation, question-and-answer sessions, intervention with individuals and groups, marking work and setting tests and tasks). They keep a variety of formats for recording their assessments to help them summarise achievements at the end of the year. It is not necessary for teachers to assess every learning objective, for every child, and to record all that they assess. Often, the outcomes from assessment will be used immediately to adjust teaching and further recording would serve no useful purpose.

In some schools teachers meet in year teams to share work (for example, children's writing), to moderate judgements and check their consistency in applying the assessment criteria. These meetings can be helpful in gaining familiarity with the criteria and identifying next steps in learning.

Reports are written once a year and consultation sessions for parents are held two or three times a year. Many schools have consultations in the autumn and spring terms and a final written report in the summer, and an open evening is held for those who wish to discuss aspects of the written report. Written reports can be extensive and teachers access a wide range of assessment evidence such as examples of work and summative assessments to write them.

Preparing to teach

You might find it helpful to observe an experienced teacher with his or her class so that you can begin to identify formative assessment taking place in the classroom. If 'assessment for learning' is happening in a classroom, you may see some of the following features.

- Clear learning objectives/intentions shared visually and verbally with children at the beginning of the lesson to enable them to know the journey they are to take. These become a reference point for the teacher and children to use, both during the lesson and in the plenary, to check progress in learning.

- Children involved in self-assessment. This can be carried out by asking children to indicate (with thumbs up or down) whether they feel confident in meeting objectives. Alternatively the whiteboard is marked with traffic lights – green, red or yellow – and children are encouraged to put one traffic light colour at the end of their work.

- Teacher intervention with individuals and groups, and questioning, becoming sharper and focused towards the achievement of objectives rather than focused on task completion. Mistakes and misconceptions are easier to identify and teachers have a clear view of how to plan the next lesson.

- Children being asked to shape the criteria for achieving the objective. For example, what they think they should achieve by the end of the lesson, what would constitute a good piece of work or how they could show they had completed the learning and met the objective.

- Children being asked to convey their understanding in a variety of ways. For example, through drawings, examination of artefacts, role play, concept mapping and initial brainstorms, and asking children to explain problems.

- Appropriate feedback being given through written comments. In marking and responding to children's work, the teacher might comment on achievement in relation to the planned learning objectives, and indicate what needs to be done to improve. When appropriate, the teacher suggests how the child can 'close the gap' (Clarke, 2001) .

Lessons are generally constructed around a 'three-part framework' with a starter/introduction, development of the main theme (which could include individual and group working) and a plenary. During the introduction the teacher may model ideas or approaches or strategies and involve children in sharing their ideas. Having a clear understanding of process and expectations is one way in which children can be supported in their learning.

Most teachers will spend time observing children before making considered interventions to individuals and groups to question children: listening to how they describe their work and inviting children to share their reasoning. Open questions are used to invite children to explore their ideas and reasoning. The literacy and numeracy strategies have impacted positively on the use of questioning by teachers to adjust lesson delivery, to check children's understanding and to sharpen subsequent questions, offer support and adapt tasks and resources accordingly. Teachers will stop individuals, groups or the whole class to revisit, clarify or extend learning if they consider some children are experiencing difficulties or a majority are ready for the next step. One recent innovation is the 'show me' board (small A4 whiteboards) which enables the teacher to obtain a response from every child. This maximises involvement and motivation and enables the teacher to see instantly which children are having difficulty with a question.

In subjects such as physical education, art and design, and music, teachers may encourage children to share ideas and opinions constructively, reflect on their own performance and identify potential for development. For example, in dance or gymnastics children can be encouraged to work in groups to apply their developing skills to shape a series of movements into a performance. Their peers could be invited to identify features which they think are successful. The teacher may encourage children to consider the ideas they have seen and to revise their own sequence.

You may wish to adapt the following list to guide your approaches to assessment, particularly during your first few months in school.

1. Ask for the school's policy on assessment, recording and reporting and for marking and responding to children's work. This should give you the school's philosophy – purposes and principles – and clear guidelines on what is expected, together with examples of proformas for recording.

2. Ask for the assessment timetable for your year group and the school as a whole. This will provide dates for internal tests, including standardised tests, optional or statutory National Tests, consultation evenings with parents and due dates for written reports.

3. Meet with the staff responsible for different aspects of assessment in the school, including the special educational needs co-ordinator (SENCO). These teachers will support you in assessing children's work and give guidance on school procedures.

4. Ask if there is a 'tracking and monitoring form' for your class. Most schools have established class tracking forms (usually computer based for ease of transfer) to identify current levels of attainment for each child in reading, writing, mathematics and, in some schools, science.

5. Look at the medium-term plans for guidance on formative assessment. There should be a column for assessment opportunities within the medium-term plan. Information may include ideas for assessment activities and should include reference to assessment criteria (i.e. National Curriculum level descriptions).

It is likely that, for some subjects, you will be encouraged to undertake some 'snapshot' assessment towards the end of a unit of work to clarify or confirm the progress children have made. The assessment may be a project, an investigation, enquiry or a problem to be resolved. It should be related to the National Curriculum level descriptors. If the school is using the QCA schemes of work, the criteria may be expressed in terms of 'expectations'.

For planned assessment within English and mathematics, you will find guidance in the National Literacy and Numeracy Strategy documents.

6. Find out if the school uses the QCA document *Keeping Track: Effective Ways of Recording Pupil Achievement to Help Raise Standards* (1999a). This gives a clear framework for recording which makes a distinction between daily/weekly records (linked to lesson plans), termly records (linked to units/schemes of work) and annual records (linked to monitoring progress and reporting).

7. Decide on strategies for recording the assessments you plan to make. You may be guided by school directives, QCA guidance, advice from colleagues and previous experience. It may be helpful to remember 'fitness for purpose' and to have a range of methods to suit different needs. Be prepared to adapt as your teaching experience progresses. Annotating your lesson plan may be enough. Equally, there can be different procedures for recording progress in different subjects: different nature of the subject, different approaches to assessment, different needs for information and alternative records (e.g. child's workbook containing marked work and instructive comments and showing progress over time).

8. Check to see whether samples of assessed work need to be kept for moderation or to exemplify standards.

Recording assessment

You may find the forms given here as Figures 6.1 – 6.5 provide useful ideas when deciding how to record assessments.

- Figure 6.1 is an individual pupil profile which can be used to support reporting.

- Figure 6.2 is a checklist for a group investigation.

- Figure 6.3 is a combination of class record and focus group, but it could be adapted for class group only. Such a form is usually coded for 'not achieved' 'okay/with help' and 'achieved', but it should not be made too complex.

- Figure 6.4 can be used for whole-class monitoring. It is suitable, for example, for skills being developed over several weeks, and could involve pupil self-recording.

- Figure 6.5 is a planning, briefing and recording sheet for teaching assistants. This could be simplified but is based on the National Numeracy Strategy.

NAME: Lauren

SPEAKING & LISTENING (General)

Able to participate in group presentation and able to defend point of view.

READING & WRITING (Literacy)

Imaginative writing. Able to write from another person's point of view.

Mostly accurate spelling.

ICT

Can enter data into a spreadsheet.

Can use internet to do own research.

NUMERACY

Quick recall of multiplication facts.

Accurate mental calculations. Finds it hard to work out what sums to do within a problem, but is v. capable to do the calculations.

SCIENCE

An interest and curiosity in the world around.

Understands and can explain concepts such as day & night, and phases of the moon.

HISTORY

Perceptive, so spots differences between schools today and in Victorian times

RE

Can think what different aspects of Christianity symbolise.

ART/DT

Careful use of clay. Created realistic, accurate Victorian clay model. Design work is neat and detailed.

MUSIC

Interesting ideas. Works well in a group to compose using a given rhythm. Performs with good sense of rhythm.

Involved in extra-curricular choir.

PE/GAMES

Running & jumping (in Athletics) v. competent. knows how to use her arms, legs and body to increase distance & height of jumps.

PSHE

Considers others.

Is aware of her rights and responsibilities.

Figure 6.1 Individual pupil profile

Parachutes assessment

Names	Fair Test	Objectives				Notes
		Know what to measure	Choose an instrument (prob.)	Make accurate measurements	Check measurement by repeating	
Richard	✓	✓	✓	✓	✗	Know he could repeat exp. but didn't want to bother really
James	✓	✗	✓	✓	✗	What to measure
Ryan	✓	✓	✓	✓	✗	Didn't see any need to repeat
Adam	✓	✓	✓	✗	✗	Needed help to use stopwatch
Melanie	✓	✓	✓	✓	✗	Wanted to repeat exp. with more time to check results
Michelle	✓	✓	✓	✓	✗	Needed help with measuring & didn't see any need for repeat
Vikki	✓	✓	✓	✓	✗	Didn't see any need to repeat

Figure 6.2 Checklist for group investigation

Subject_____   Date_____

Learning Objectives (cross-referenced to Lesson Plan)
1._____
2._____
3._____

Pupil	1	2	3	Pupil	1	2	3

Figure 6.3 Class record/focus group

ICT Assessment Sheet

KEY • Independent/ confident < Minimal support/reminder --- 1-2-1 support	COMMUNICATING				CONTROL		ADVENTURE SIMULATIONS		SAVING AND PRINTING	
	Navigate keyboard to find appropriate letters and control keys	Be aware of differences between lower and upper case; changing appropriately	Use return key to start a new line	Can change size and colour of text	Can recognise that everyday devices (tape recorders etc) respond to signals and commands to control them	Can control roamer; clear memory, move forwards and backwards, turn left and right	Can navigate CD-ROM programs	Can change/load pre-installed CD-ROM program	Can print own work independently	Can save work onto hard-drive/into file

Figure 6.4 Whole class monitoring

Lesson: Subject_____ **Date:**_____

Name of classroom assistant or additional adult working with the group:

| **Activity:** |
| *Brief account of the activity and the intended focus* |
| **Resources:** |
| **Words to use:** |
| *Key vocabulary to be used by adult and introduced to pupils* |
| *Key questions to be used* |

Key Objectives/Learning Points:

1.

2.

3.

Children's names		Can do	Needs help	Note: Difficulties or issues when planning next level of support
	1			
	2			
	3			
	1			
	2			
	3			
	1			
	2			
	3			
	1			
	2			
	3			

Figure 6.5 Planning, briefing and recording

Summary

- Improving pupil progression and performance is an essential aspect of primary teaching.

- Recent research suggests formative rather than summative assessment improves performance.

- Formative assessment has become known as 'assessment for learning'.

- 'Assessment for learning' involves actively involving children in the assessment process.

- Each school has an individual assessment policy.

Useful resources

Assessment Reform Group (2002) *Assessment for Learning: 10 Principles*. Cambridge: Cambridge University School of Education.

Black, P and Wiliam, D (1998) *Inside the Black Box. Raising Standards through Classroom Assessment*. London: King's College.

Black, P and Wiliam, D (1998) Assessment and classroom learning. *Assessment in Education Journal*, 5(1), pp. 7–11.

Black, P, Harrison, C, Lee, C, Marshall, B and Wiliam, D (2002) *Working inside the black box: assessment for learning in the classroom*. London: King's College.

Clarke, S (1998) *Targeting Assessment in the Primary Classroom*. London: Hodder & Stoughton.

Clarke, S (2001) *Unlocking Formative Assessment*. London: Hodder & Stoughton.

Harlen, W (2001) *Teaching, Learning and Assessing Science 5–12*. London: Paul Chapman.

This chapter will:

→ discuss changes in methods and styles of managing behaviour in the primary school;

→ give information on the type of behaviour policies and practice that you are likely to encounter in the primary school;

→ give practical suggestions to help you manage behaviour.

Background reading

To help you understand current practice regarding behaviour management, you should gain access to copies of the following documentation: *The National Curriculum: Handbook for Primary Teachers in England* (DfEE, 1999b) – look at the framework for personal, social and health education and citizenship – *Social Inclusion: Pupil Support* (DfEE, 1999g) and *Special Educational Needs: Code of Practice* (DfES, 2002) – look in particular at Section 7.60 in relation to behaviour.

Copies can be accessed via websites or ordered by telephone, fax or e-mail. Details are given at the end of this chapter.

Also try to obtain copies of school behaviour policies. These can usually be found in school prospectuses. Look for statements about the school ethos, rewards and sanctions.

Background

When I speak to teachers returning to the profession they often tell me that their main concern is behaviour management. This may be because of the high profile that school behaviour has in the media. It may also be because fear of losing control affects self-belief and can consequently undermine a positive attitude necessary in returning to the classroom.

Change in society has frequently been cited as the reason for disruptive behaviour. However, the issue often evolves around whether children are seen as the problem or their behaviour. Home and school environments are very different and, accordingly, demand different behaviour. Factors such as teacher expectation, class management style and school ethos can have more influence on behaviour than a child's home background. Of course, home circumstances are often reflected in the behaviour of the child in school but frequently the school is the most secure, stable environment a child with problems at home may have.

The amount of change in the practice of managing behaviour will obviously vary according to when you last taught in school. The Elton Report (DES, 1989c) was influential in changing practice and its effect is still evident in practice today. It was set up following concerns about behaviour in schools. It looked at a wide range of factors and made recommendations. A positive school ethos was seen as paramount to promoting good behaviour. The Elton Report identified such factors as school management style, behaviour policies, the curriculum, school environment and identification of the role of parents as key elements in developing the school ethos.

During the last ten years more children who would have been educated in special schools now attend mainstream schools. Consequently, you may find yourself surprised by the diverse needs of children you are to teach. The focus today is on inclusion, not just for those with learning or physical difficulties but also for those who demonstrate social, emotional or behavioural difficulties. The teacher must make the curriculum accessible to all. This can be challenging but it is essential. If not it may lead to poor self-esteem in a child, boredom, lack of self-motivation and consequently behaviour problems.

Current practice

Schools are very active in monitoring behaviour. They are required to audit behaviour, set targets for improvement and put in place strategies to meet these targets. Local education authorities (LEAs) must assist schools in this process and are required to make arrangements for the education of children with behaviour difficulties. The aim is to keep exclusion of children from school to a minimum.

The current policy is contained in DfEE Circular 10/99 (DfEE, 1999f). Essentially there are no targets for exclusion for LEAs. New guidance gives governors greater powers to exclude and subsequently exclusions nationally have risen again. Guidance now states:

> . . . the governing body and the headteacher are responsible for promoting good behaviour and discipline on behalf of the schools pupils and for securing an orderly and safe environment for pupils and staff.

> DfEE, 1999

This obviously leads to a wide interpretation of what constitutes an orderly and safe environment and heads are interpreting this in many ways. However, the new guidance goes on to say:

> . . . responses to pupils displaying challenging behaviour must be made in the context of the schools behaviour policy and should encompass a range of strategies with exclusion as one option so that the interests of the whole school are reflected in the action taken.

This can be a concern to LEAs who feel governing bodies and head teachers could use the guidance as a licence to exclude. It later states, however, that exclusion should only be used as a last resort when all other strategies have been tried. For the first time there is guidance where a serious circumstance might result in a permanent exclusion, even if a first offence. The offences listed are:

- actual or threatened violence against staff or pupils;

- sexual misconduct;

- supplying an illegal drug;

- carrying an offensive weapon.

All the above are again open to wide interpretation. For example, a compass could be an offensive weapon if misused.

In addition to the above there are now sections on lunchtime exclusion (where a parent has the right to make representation to a discipline committee), children in public care who are high risk in underachieving and police involvement and parallel criminal proceedings.

Practice varies from school to school but there are some factors that are fairly consistent. First, a behaviour policy will be in place reflecting the ethos of the school. The statement about the ethos will identify such factors as courtesy, co-operation and kindness. School rules will be included and are usually written in a form that is understood by all the children and all the teaching and ancillary staff. They will identify expectations of behaviour. Procedures will be outlined when the standard of behaviour is considered to fall below the school's expectations with a statement on rewards and sanctions. Usually there will be a separate statement on bullying and physical restraint. It is common practice to involve and gain the support of parents in behaviour management by developing clear communication between home and school. Schools usually require parents to sign home–school agreements as evidence of accepting the policies of the school.

You may be familiar with behaviour modification programmes such as the ABC (antecedent, behaviour, consequence) of behaviour. This method is still used with children with severe behavioural difficulties and is founded on a behaviourist perspective based on work such as that of Skinner. First, the event that preceded the behaviour (the antecedent) is identified. The consequence to the behaviour is based on positive consequences increasing the behaviour and negative responses decreasing the behaviour. As an example, if hitting another child results in removal from the setting then, if the child dislikes this, behaviour may be modified as hitting will be associated with removal. It must be remembered that a consequence can be negative to one child but positive to another (e.g. the child may like being removed from the setting).

In recent years some schools have adopted what has been called assertive discipline. It is one behaviour management technique mentioned in the White Paper *Excellence in Schools* (DfEE, 1998a). This approach sets clear rules, gives continuous positive feedback when children keep to these rules and offers a hierarchy of sanctions which are applied in sequence when rules are broken, such as first warning the child about inappropriate behaviour, writing the child's name on the board, and then removing the child from the group. The ultimate sanction would be exclusion from school but this is never lightly undertaken.

The formal curriculum contributes to raising standards of behaviour. Personal, social and health education (PSHE) and citizenship are a requirement in the National Curriculum. The same care needs to be given to this area of the curriculum as to others. There should be a programme of study, plans and assessment opportunities and resources available.

Praise is an important part of most behaviour management. The purpose is to reinforce good behaviour rather than emphasise poor behaviour. Praise can be for listening, trying hard, being prepared, helping the teacher/other child, not just for doing a piece of work well. An individual child's targets will vary and therefore praise will be given accordingly.

Rewards and sanctions are only successful when they are applied consistently by all in the school and the system has been clearly communicated to children and parents. Such approaches emphasise that it is the behaviour that is been objected to, not the child. They aim to develop the child's ability to accept responsibility for his or her actions yet, at the same, time not to undermine self-esteem.

Preparing to teach

As a professional you need to understand not just what to do but why you are doing it. This partly depends on the role you believe a teacher should have in the school. Are you authoritarian or more democratic and how does this relate to your teaching and management style?

Coupled with your personal view will be that of the school in which you will teach. Although you will eventually have a role in defining policy, initially you will have to work within a policy to which you did not contribute. Consequently, reflecting upon your style when you were last teaching is a good way forward to making sense of changes in practice in behaviour management. The aim must be to find a solution to behaviour issues that allows teaching and learning to take place effectively

Which of the following statements do you believe about the role of the teacher?

- The teacher has a right and responsibility to be in charge.

- The teacher has a right to control children.

- The teacher controls but consults with children.

- The teacher aims to avert behaviour problems but at times has to control.

- The teacher and the pupils have equal rights to have their needs met.

You could view these statements as part of a continuum with an authoritarian approach at one side and democratic one at the other. You may believe that the role of the teacher varies according to the age, background and specific needs of children. However, try to consider where you roughly fit into this continuum. If you veer towards the authoritarian approach you may think that children should not be praised for behaving well or that assertive behaviour policies are the best ways forward. If you feel that meeting a child's needs is paramount then you may feel more comfortable with a more democratic approach.

It is also useful to apply this idea of a continuum to your teaching style. Do you see your teaching as the main means by which children learn, or do you believe to a greater or lesser extent that children learn, through experience and when their emotional needs have been met? Try not to mix approaches in teaching and managing. Children will become confused if you elicit and acknowledge their opinions on acceptable behaviour in the classroom and then teach in a didactic manner or vice versa. Obviously, you will not be free to manage behaviour and teach exactly in the way you want, as you will have to adhere to both government and school policy. However, consideration of these issues may help you make sense of changes you encounter.

The school

Obtain a copy of the school's behaviour policy. Internalise the school's approach at the outset and apply it consistently. No teacher is alone with behaviour problems. To admit help is needed is not an admission of failure. Problems should not be treated simply as personal issue but as an aspect of professional development. Find out the chain of support that is available.

The classroom

A well ordered, pleasant environment created by you says a great deal about who is in charge of the room. Consider tidiness, organisation of resources, safety, displays, furniture layout and seating arrangements. Everyone responds better when his or her environment is pleasant. The teacher and children's working environment is mainly the classroom. Displays are a way of enhancing learning, valuing children's work as well as making the classroom attractive.

Classrooms need to be adaptable to a range of curriculum subjects. With the introduction of the literacy and numeracy strategies there came a need for all children to be able to sit on the floor. As time has moved on this idea has been adapted as many schools had insufficient space for this without the children becoming overcrowded. Also some schools have acknowledged that sitting for a period of time (such as 20 minutes) on the floor can be uncomfortable and lead to children losing concentration. You have to decide what is the most effective layout for your particular classroom. Sitting in a horseshoe shape has often been found to be beneficial for teaching and learning but rarely are classrooms large enough to accommodate this arrangement.

Children often like to have a place to call their own. It gives them a sense of security and belonging. Consider carefully the idea of not allocating specific places to children. Similarly, constantly changing seating arrangements can unsettle many children. If you do feel a change is required try to discuss this with the children and gain their views. In this way they will feel more in control of the changing environment and positive about it.

The children

Just as we expect children to work hard and behave well to earn our respect, so they expect the same of their teachers. A child's teacher needs to be a good role model, consistent, fair and trustworthy. Standards in teaching have, since the introduction of Office for Standards in Education (OFSTED) inspections, had an increasingly high profile and pupil expectations have risen accordingly. Standards of behaviour often reflect the standards of the teaching in terms of organisation, planning, differentiation, subject knowledge and pedagogy.

Lessons

Circle time is common in primary schools today and is an opportunity to develop a positive classroom ethos and to build self-esteem. It gives the pupils and teacher a chance to build a team, sharing issues of behaviour without personalising them. Ground rules need to be set such as allowing everyone to speak who wants to and only one person speaking at a time. Children should not be pressured to contribute but all should listen and respect an individual's contribution. At the beginning of the school year it is a good way of devising class rules. Once they are drawn up and displayed by the teacher and pupils together they have common ownership and can be a means of children understanding any sanctions imposed when a rule is broken. As children get older class councils, learning logs and personal journals all give pupils the chance to air their views and suggest ways of supporting and improving behavioural difficulties.

Planning

Just as you need to plan to teach so planning needs to be in place to promote good behaviour. Consider any potential problems when children are likely to be more disruptive such as moving in the room or using a particular resource. In this way negative behaviour can be pre-empted or diffused.

The literacy and numeracy strategies have required teachers to make explicit the learning objectives for each lesson as it is believed that to teach effectively children have to understand the purpose of the lesson and by so doing will respond positively. Some schools use specific strategies to ensure that children really understand these objectives and require teachers to use them. One example is the use of phrases such as 'What I'm looking for' (WILF) and 'That is because' (TIB) for each lesson. The aim is to put objectives and purpose in child-friendly language.

The teaching assistant

You need to know both the learning and emotional needs of all the children in your class. In a class of 30 children with ever-changing needs this is not easy. Make sure you are aware of any significant factors about children in your class by looking at school records. Elicit the help of other adults in the class. Many primary classes now have the support of a teaching assistant for at least part of the day. They often develop close relationships with children and can provide a valuable insight into the cause of behavioural difficulties. They are also often able to pre-empt difficulty. They can quickly notice if work set is too hard for the child, that a necessary resource is not available or that an individual is having a bad day.

Class rewards and sanctions

Whatever rewards and sanctions you use in the class they must fit into school system. Team points, sticker charts, certificates, and 'golden time' are popular rewards. Class treats such as extra playtime and special food are popular and valuable motivators. Sanctions may include withdrawal of privileges or giving tasks in a child's free time, such as break time. 'Time-out' can be a successful strategy for diffusing behaviour when a child is having difficulty behaving. This is not to be confused with exclusion. It involves such strategies as the teaching assistant taking a child for a walk or giving a child a different individual task to do for a short period of time.

Teacher talk

As has already been stated the use of praise and rewards is part of most behaviour management policies. When returning to the classroom some teachers find it difficult to phrase responses to children positively. Usually this is achieved by rephrasing a command into an explanatory statement so 'Stop talking' becomes ' I need you to be quiet so I can hear you answer the register'. Also praising children for behaviour that they believe should be expected can at first be difficult for some teachers. However, it reinforces expected behaviour for the whole class and is a means by which all children can be successful. Examples of such praise are 'Thank you for walking' or 'Well done for sitting quietly'. Similarly, it is useful to reconsider phrases you may have used frequently. 'Well done' and 'Good' are positive responses but they don't give children any indication of exactly why they have been praised. Attaching the reason to the praise gives it more meaning – 'Well done for using capital letters and full stops in your work today' or 'Good – you shared the pencils without any fuss'. When in school actively observe this aspect of 'teacher talk' so you are also able to respond to children in a similar manner.

Summary

- You may find children in your class who would have previously been excluded because of their difficulty in controlling behaviour.

- There has been a change in recent years from managing behaviour by punishing unacceptable behaviour to more emphasis upon identifying and praising acceptable behaviour.

- Behaviour management needs careful planning at both school and classroom level.

- Teacher assistants can play an active role in helping manage behaviour.

- Most school behaviour policies give clear guidance to teachers as well as children and parents about how behaviour is managed in the school. You must always work within the policy framework.

Useful resources

Cowley, S (2001) *Getting the Buggers to Behave*. London: Continuum.

DES/WO (1989) *Discipline in Schools: Report of the Committee of Enquiry Chaired by Lord Elton*. London: HMSO.

DfEE (1998a) *Excellence in Schools*. London: DfEE.

DfEE (1999) *The National Curriculum: Handbook for Primary Teachers in England*. London: HMSO.

DfEE (1999) *Social Inclusion: Pupil Support*. Circular 10/99. London: HMSO.

DfES (2001) *Special Educational Needs: Code of Practice*. London: HMSO.

DfES (2001) *Inclusive Schooling*. London: HMSO.

Docking, J W (1996) *Managing Behaviour in the Primary School Classroom*. London: David Fulton.

Mosely, J (1993) *Turn your School Around*. Wisbech: Learning Development Aids.

Mosely, J (1996) *Quality Circle Time*. Wisbech: Learning Development Aids.

Mosely, J (1998) *More Quality Circle Time*. Wisbech: Learning Development Aids.

OFSTED (1999) *Inspecting Schools*. London: HMSO.

Porter, L (2000) *Behaviour in Schools: Theory and Practice for Teachers*. Buckingham: Open University Press.

Rogers, B. (1997) *The Language of Discipline*. Plymouth: Northcote House Publishers.

Contact information

Copies of government documentation can be accessed via websites or ordered by telephone, fax or e-mail.

Department of Education and Skills
www.dfes.gov.uk/index.htm
Tel: 0845 60 222 60
Fax: 0845 60 333 60
e-mail: **dfes@prolog.uk.com**

National Curriculum
www.nc.uk.net
The Foundation Curriculum
www.qca.org.uk/
Tel: 01787 884444
Fax: 01787 312950

The National Numeracy and Literacy Strategy
www.dfes.standards.gov.uk/numeracy
www.dfes.standards.gov.uk/literacy
DfEE Publications
PO Box 5050
Sudbury,
Suffolk
CO10 6ZQ

Qualifications and Curriculum Authority (for assessment and reporting guidance)
www.qca.org.uk
Publications Tel: 01787 884444

References

AAIA (2000) *Pupils' Learning from Teachers' Responses.* AAIA.

Adams, M (1994) *Beginning to Read: Thinking and Learning about Print.* Cambridge, MA: MIT Press.

Alexander, R (1992) *Curriculum Organisation and Classroom Practice in Primary Schools.* London: DES.

ASE (2001) *Be Safe! Health and Safety in Primary School Science and Technology* (3rd edn). Hatfield: Association for Science Education.

Assessment Reform Group (1999) *Assessment for Learning: Beyond the Black Box.* Cambridge: Cambridge University School of Education.

Assessment Reform Group (2002) *Assessment for Learning: 10 Principles.* Cambridge: Cambridge University School of Education.

Beard, R (1999) *National Literacy Strategy: Review of Research and Related Evidence.* London: HMSO.

Bennett, L (2000) *Focus English.* Oxford: Heinemann.

Black, P and Wiliam, D (1998a) Assessment and classroom learning. *Assessment in Education Journal,* 5(1).

Black, P and Wiliam, D (1998b) *Inside the Black Box. Raising Standards through Classroom Assessment.* London: King's College.

Brooks, G (1998) Trends in literacy standards 1948–1996. *Language and Literacy News,* Spring: 3–4.

CACE (1967) *Children and their Primary Schools (the Plowden Report).* London: HMSO.

Callaway, C and Kear, M (1999) *Teaching Art and Design in the Primary School.* London: David Fulton.

Clarke, S (1998) *Targeting Assessment in the Primary Classroom.* London: Hodder & Stoughton.

Clarke, S (2001) *Unlocking Formative Assessment.* London: Hodder & Stoughton.

Clay, M (1979) *The Early Detection of Reading Difficulties.* Oxford: Heinemann.

Cockburn, A (2001) *Teaching Children 3 to 11.* London: Paul Chapman.

Crystal, D (1996) *Discover Grammar.* Harlow: Longman.

DES (1982a) *Mathematics Counts (the Cockcroft Report).* London: HMSO.

DES (1982b) *Better Schools.* London: HMSO.

DES (1989a) *English in the National Curriculum.* London: HMSO.

DES (1989b) *National Curriculum: From Policy to Practice.* London: DES.

DES (1989c) *The Elton Report.* London: HMSO.

DES (1993) *The National Curriculum and its Assessment – Interim Report.* London: DES.

DfEE (1997) *The Implementation of the National Literacy Strategy.* London: HMSO.

DfEE (1998a) *Excellence in Schools.* London: HMSO.

DfEE (1998b) *The National Literacy Strategy: Framework for Teaching.* London: HMSO.

DfEE (1999a) *Progression in Phonics.* London: HMSO.

DfEE (1999b) *The National Curriculum: Handbook for Primary Teachers in England.* London: HMSO.

DfEE (1999c) *Curriculum 2000: Handbook for Teachers.* London: HMSO.

DfEE (1999d) *The National Curriculum: Mathematics Key Stages 1 and 2.* London: HMSO.

DfEE (1999e) *National Numeracy Strategy.* London: HMSO.

DfEE (1999f) *Framework for Teaching Mathematics.* London: HMSO.

DfEE (1999g) *Social Inclusion: Pupil Support.* Circular 10/99. London: HMSO.

DfEE (2000a) *Supporting Pupils with Special Educational Needs in the Literacy Hour.* London: HMSO.

DfEE (2000b) *Grammar for Writing.* London: HMSO.

DfEE (2000c) *Handbook for Inspecting Primary and Nursery Schools.* London: HMSO.

DfEE (2001a) *Developing Early Writing.* London: HMSO.

DfEE (2001b) *Special Educational Needs: Code of Practice.* London: HMSO.

DfEE/QCA (2000) *Curriculum Guidance for the Foundation Stage.* London: DfEE/QCA.

DfES (2001) *Watching and Learning 2.* London: HMSO.

DfES (2002) *Special Educational Needs: Code of Practice.* London: HMSO.

Dillon, J T (1994) *Using Discussion in Classrooms.* Buckingham: Open University Press.

Earl, L (2001) *Watching and Learning 2.* London: HMSO.

Edwards, S (1999a) *Writing for All.* London: David Fulton.

Edwards, S (1999b) *Speaking and Listening for All.* London: David Fulton.

Edwards, S (1999c) *Reading for All.* London: David Fulton.

Ennever, L and Harlen, W (1972) *With Objectives in Mind: Guide to Science 5/13.* London: Macdonald.

Farrell, M (1999) *Key Issues for Primary Schools.* London: Routledge.

Fisher, R (2002) *Inside the Literacy Hour.* London: Routledge.

Fountas, I (1997) *Guided Reading.* Oxford: Heinemann.

Gaines, K (2000) *Handbook to the Oxford Literacy Web.* Oxford: Oxford University Press.

Galton, M, Gray, J and Rudduck, J (1999) *The Impact of School Transitions and Transfers on Pupil Progress and Attainment. DfEE Research Report* RR131. London: HMSO.

Goldsworthy, A, Watson, R and Wood-Robinson, V (2000) *Targeted Learning.* A KSIS Report. London: ASE/King's College.

Graves, D (1983) *Writing: Teachers and Children at Work.* Oxford: Heinemann.

Harlen, W (1985) *Taking the Plunge.* London: Heinemann.

Harlen, W (2001) *Teaching, Learning and Assessing Science 5–12.* London: Paul Chapman.

Hayes, L (2001) *Am I Teaching Well?* Exeter: Learning Matters.

HIAS (2000) *Challenging Able Children: A Handbook for Primary Schools.* Hants CC.

HMI (1978) *Primary Education in England.* London: HMSO.

HMI (1985) *The Curriculum 5–16.* London: HMSO.

HMI (2002) *Subject Report: Science.* London: OFSTED.

Hobsbaum, A (2002) *Guiding Reading.* London: London Institute of Education.

Holdaway, D (1979) *The Foundations of Literacy.* Leamington Spa: Aston Scholastic.

Holmes, E (1999) *Handbook for Newly Qualified Teachers.* London: HMSO.

Hughes, P (2000) *Principles of Primary Education: Study Guide.* London: David Fulton.

IAEP (1998) *Concentrating on Numeracy* – a keynote address presented at the Portsmouth Local Education Authority Numeracy Conference. 8 December 1998.

Jacques, K (2000) *Professional Studies Primary Phase.* Exeter: Learning Matters.

James, M and Gipps, C (1998) Broadening the basis of assessment to prevent the narrowing of learning. *The Curriculum Journal,* 9 (3) pp. 285–297.

Lazim, A (2000) *Choosing Texts for the National Literacy Strategy.* London: CLPE.

Medwell, J (2000) *The Oxford Literacy Web: Launch into Literacy.* Oxford: Oxford University Press.

Medwell, J (2002) *Primary English Knowledge and Understanding.* Exeter: Learning Matters.

NACCCE (1999) *All our Futures: Creativity, Culture and Education.* London: DfES.

National Numeracy Strategy (1999) *Assessment*. London: DfEE.

Naylor, S and Keogh, B (2000) *Concept Cartoons in Science Education*. Sandbach: Millgate House Publishers.

Nuffield Primary Science (1993a) *Key Stage I: Introduction and Index*. London: Collins Educational.

Nuffield Primary Science (1993b) *Key Stage II: Introduction and Index*. London: Collins Educational.

OFSTED (1998) *The Arts Inspected*. London: HMSO.

OFSTED (1999) *The National Literacy Strategy: An Evaluation of the First Year*. London: HMSO.

OFSTED (2001) *Primary Subject Report for Art and Design*. London: HMSO.

OFSTED (2002) *Subject Report: Science*. London: HMSO.

Phinn, G (2000) *Young Readers and their Books*. London: David Fulton.

Poole, P (2001) *Primary ICT Handbook: English*. Cheltenham: Nelson Thornes.

QCA (1998) *Vocabulary Book* London: HMSO.

QCA (1998a) *Maintaining Breadth and Balance at Key Stages 1 and 2*. London: QCA.

QCA (1998b) *Science: A Scheme of Work for Key Stages 1 and 2*. London: QCA.

QCA (1999) *Developing the School Curriculum*. London: DfEE/QCA p.21.

QCA (1999a) *Keeping Track. Effective Way of Recording Pupil Achievement to Help Raise Standards*. London: QCA.

QCA (1999b) *Target Setting and Assessment in the National Literacy Strategy*. London: QCA.

QCA (2000) *The Curriculum Guidance for the Foundation Stage*. London: HMSO.

QCA (2002) *Designing and Timetabling the Primary Curriculum – a Practical Guide for Key Stages 1 and 2*. London: HMSO.

QCA (2002) Designing and timetabling the Primary Curriculum, London, DfEE/QCA.

Richards, C (2000) *Changing English Primary Education*. Stoke on Trent: Trentham.

Rose, A (1997) *Collins Grammar Rules*. London: Collins.

Rowling, J (1997) *Harry Potter and the Philosopher's Stone*. London: Bloomsbury.

Sadler, D R (1998) Feedback to students: an analysis. *Assessment in Education Journal*, 5(1) pp. 77–84.

Seuss, D (1958) *The Cat in the Hat*. London: Collins.

Smith, F (1978) *Reading*. Cambridge: Cambridge University Press.

Southgate, V (1981) *Extending Beginning Reading*. Oxford: Heinemann.

TGAT (1988) *National Curriculum Task Group on Assessment and Testing: A Report*. London: DES.

TTA (2000) *Supporting Assessment for the Award of QTS: Year 6 Classrooms*. London: TTA.

TTA (2002) *Specification for a Contract to Run Returners' Courses*. London: TTA.

Wastenedge, E R (1967) *Nuffield Junior Science: Teachers' Guides I and II*. London: Collins.

White, E (1952) *Charlotte's Web*. London: Hamilton.

INDEX